The Hero
of
Blind Pig Island

and Other Island Stories

Novels by Jimmy Olsen

Things In Ditches

Poison Makers

The Hero
of
Blind Pig Island

and Other Island Stories

Jimmy Olsen

Hoffman House
PRESS

Hoffman House
PRESS

505 Fourth Street South
P.O. Box 161
Hoffman, MN 56339

First Hoffman House Press softcover original edition August, 2012

This book is also available as an eBook on Kindle, Nook, and iPad Go to www.hoffmanhousepress.com for further information.

Cover photograph from: Macduff Everton.
                           MandM Inc.
                           3905 State Street #7-213
                           Santa Barbara, CA 93105

Manufactured in the United States of America

Olsen, Jimmy

   The Hero of Blind Pig Island And Other Stories/by Jimmy Olsen
      First Hoffman House Press edition

Contact Hoffman House Press: www.hoffmanhousepress.com
or Email hoffmanhousepress@cloudnet.com
Jimmy Olsen: www.jimmyolsen.net

ISBN 978-0-9801835-6-6

Table of Contents

The Hero
of
Blind Pig Island
and Other Island Stories

Party Girl

To get to Dale Sterling's house I had to drive right by the spot where they assassinated Trujillo. It wasn't marked, but everyone knew it. I was squeamish passing there – the old Jefe's blood soaked into the limestone, the weeds it watered left untended, but I had a backseat loaded with party supplies for Sterling and it was a pretty day. Hot, as late summer days can be. They named streets after Trujillo's assassins now, so I passed by, arm resting on the window, eyeing a solitary osprey that dipped and soared on the thermals along the cliffs above an aquamarine sea, and thought no more about it.

Dr. Sterling was the school administrator giving the party for the new hires. My favorite party of the season and our first chance to examine the fresh meat. We took bets on them. Which new teachers would fold by Christmas, Easter, or make it nine months. They landed with juvenile optimism and their Caribbean dreams seemed to us silly enough to make them pitiable, but in time we just thought them immature, and snickered behind their backs and paid off our bets. We were right most of the time, too. Few ever made it more than a year. The 1970s were primitive times there.

I slid the last of the grocery bags onto Sterling's dining room table and he said, "You didn't forget the pear juice? It's the secret to my punch. Plenty of pear juice."

"I got it."

"Good. I'll read, you mix. Unless you have to get going?"

"No," I said. "I can stay and give you a hand." He was alone in a big old house half out in the country along the San Cristóbal Highway. Last place on earth I'd have picked to live. He told me he rented it so his wife could entertain. Sterling had been there three years. His wife never showed up. I didn't pry. He always seemed very perky and pleasant. We wondered about her though.

"The secret to a good punch," Dale Sterling was saying, "is pear juice. You got to hide the bite of the booze and smooth it out, you know? That's why you need the pear juice. Pear juice can hide a gallon of booze and make you think you're drinking pure fruit juice. You'll see."

I can't say that I liked or disliked Dale Sterling. I'd lost the bet on him when he came but we kept it quiet that we bet on administrators as well as teachers. But in fact, administrators were usually older and when they came face to face with the Third World for the first time, the reaction was often more violent and entertaining than the reactions of the younger teachers. Many of the teachers were single, while the administrators usually had husbands or wives to bet on too.

"There's a couple pretty ones," Sterling was saying. "One of them is short but she's stacked and never wears a bra."

"What? Who are you talking about?"

"The new teachers."

"How do you know what they look like? Nobody's seen them yet."

"New policy. Mr. Cromwell assigned me to welcome all the new teachers at the airport and bring them to town. Even gives me the guaguita and a chauffeur."

"I'll be damned," I said. "That was my idea. I've been after the old fart for years, ever since I came here and ended up forty miles from town in some beachfront hotel at thirty-eight bucks a night. Bitched and bitched. Said he couldn't waste the manpower to babysit new hires."

"Well, he's wasting mine." Sterling smiled. "But it's not bad duty. I'm the first friendly, English-speaking face they see."

"And there you are, looking at their boobs."

"Somebody has to do it."

I lined the bottles up along the dining room table. "What did we get, besides stacked short women?" I asked.

"Here's the bowl," he said, placing an extremely large crystal piece on the table. "I'll read the recipe, you pour it in. Let's see. We got the junior high math teacher. She has a limp. Some guy to take Fey's place. Looks boring as hell. The Latinos will hate him. There's two more divorcees from Texas. I think everybody in Texas has changed partners. A guy who got off the plane drunk. He's teaching sixth grade. Told me he was a gambler. He'll be broke by Thanksgiving. A married couple – that's a twofer. Cromwell loves those. She's social studies and he's science, I think. They're here for an adventure before they settle down and have kids. Let's see. Oh yeah, a tall girl who talked about her pastor all the way back to town."

"Must've been hard on you. Wasn't she stacked? Are you going to read the recipe?"

"Yes," he said. "She had a body like Ann Margaret, but taller, more leggy. Head like Joan Crawford. Very serious. No nonsense. No party girl. Three quarts guava and two quarts of 7up."

I poured.

"Two quarts rum."

"Two?"

"Hey, I'm just following the recipe." Dale Sterling smiled again.

He had one off-color tooth in the front row. It was almost hidden by his white mustache, but not well enough. "What they don't know doesn't hurt 'em."

I made a mental note to mix my own drinks and keep Patricia away from the punch. She liked a good punch.

Sterling was reading, "One quart Southern Comfort."

"I thought this was fruit punch?"

"Two quarts pear juice! There you go. Fruit."

"What's left?"

"Two quarts orange, one quart papaya, the juice of fifty fresh squeezed limes already in the refrigerator, some coconut milk if we have it, which I don't, and grenadine for color." He folded the list and placed it back inside a metal recipe box with a flowered cover. "Got all that?"

"Yep," I said, pouring two-handed. "Won't catch me drinking any of this concoction."

Sterling produced two stubby glasses and a dipper. "Try it," he said.

It was smooth. Tasted exactly like fruit punch. No hint of alcohol. "Well?" he asked.

"Wouldn't of believed it."

Dale Sterling emptied his glass. "Refreshing too," he said. "It's the pear juice. It'll lay them out like Norwegian cod."

We almost didn't make it to that party. Our four year old was throwing up and Patricia worried it wasn't fair to leave the maid alone with her, and the baby too. That was fine with me but in the end the maid was offended we didn't trust her to handle things, so we went.

I drove a British sedan in those days. It looked like a gray gangster car from the 1930s. The new hires came with Filiberto, the school chauffeur. He brought them in one of the guaguitas, the VW or the Japanese one. The VW that night. I saw them arrive and was one of the first to memorize their names. A trick of mine. I won a bet once because the guy I bet with had mixed up the names and bet on the wrong elementary teacher. Sixty pesos. Nothing to sneeze at. Almost forty bucks. I use various scientific memory techniques to remember names. Barbara, the one without her bra, was Brabra. It worked. The gambler was Lucas – cool hand Luke. The one who talked about her pastor was Pricilla – Prissy Preacher. I knew every one of them before they got to the punch bowl.

Dale Sterling had pretty good taste in music and managed to get by with some fairly recent stuff without anybody complaining. That's a tough order with a room filled with school board members, pompous administrators, embassy pukes and missionaries. He swore the punch was non-alcoholic too. It sure looked like it was going to be quite a night.

Everybody dressed to the hilt, of course. Latino culture in those days had the perfect dress code. Men wore guayaberas, pressed slacks and polished shoes shined by somebody else. Women adorned themselves in any kind of fantastic creation they found on the island or in Miami. They cut out the backs or fronts of their dresses, slit the skirts, drug them on the floor, strapped them or unstrapped them, tied them, ribboned them. Thick material or sleek as seal skins - didn't matter. Lots of color or none at all. Fiesta all the time, and small wonder we danced while our kids puked. Even the missionary women wore floor length gowns and open-toed heels. Prissy Pricilla had on the best creation, I thought. A floral number with four more inches of cleavage than she'd intended. She yanked the dress down at the waist from time to time to tighten the cleavage gap but thankfully it didn't work very well.

I was having a great time. People were milling around, commenting favorably on the non-alcoholic punch. Some were already back for seconds, including Pricilla. She was nervous and sitting beside one of the more stilted missionaries and his wife. I knew the wife. She had big feet and an aversion to Truman Capote.

I had my senior high students read his new book *In Cold Blood*
the year before. In some ways I actually agreed with her about the
book, and it didn't represent Capote's best work either, but I taught
it another year just to show her I could. Dumb, really.

María Postego taught eighth grade Spanish. She was Cuban and
her ex-husband was Dominican. She posted the largest bets and
usually won them. She'd been there for years and had a good eye
for weakness. She liked to snuggle. "Don't be so obvious, Clive,"
she said in my ear. "Soon enough I will take your money." She
kissed my cheek.

"Not this time," I said.

"You are staring at the one on the couch with the missionaries."
She nodded. "Very poised. Hair up. Did she do it herself, I wonder?
She has what you say, the nice boobies?"

"María. Shame on you. How pedestrian and crude." I sipped my
rum. "She's had two glasses of Sterling's punch and she's built like
a brick shithouse."

"Hmm. Ten says she's gone by Christmas."

"I'll take it. She's carrying more weight than you think. Big boned
and strong. I'm going to guess she's Midwestern. Maybe even a
farm girl. Grew up tossing bales and milking. She's just here on
vacation."

"Sucker," María said.

"Forget ten," I countered. "I want twenty."

María studied the girl for awhile longer. "She's nervous," she said,
shaking her head.

"I'm nervous with that Longstocking woman, or whatever her
name is."

"That's not her name it's the name of her religion."

"There's no longstocking religion," I told her.

She studied the girl again. "Okay," she said finally. "I'll take it for
twenty. Pesos or dollars?"

"Pesos of course. Do I look like a millionaire?"

Most years, some time between eleven o'clock and midnight, the missionaries and board members filtered out and things got going. Latino music dominated and most everyone danced awhile, then off to other parties or discos along the Malecón until breakfast. We tried to do that five days a week if we had the energy. But by ten o'clock that night Pricilla was noticeably drunk on pear juice punch and the missionaries had allowed her a little extra room on the couch. She was talking in a loud but proper voice and periodically staring aghast at her own heaving cleavage. María found me again and said she'd go thirty but I declined.

I thought about putting Prissy wise to the punch but I'd never won by cheating. She got to pouring the stuff down like sluice water and it was all I could do to leave her alone.

Somewhere around eleven, before the older crowd left, Pricilla Johnson passed out with her head on the longstocking woman's shoulder and her slack mouth set in an inebriated grin. Someone had stuck a single red rose from the dining room bouquet between her folded fingers, and across the room María Postego rubbed her hands together to illustrate her accumulating wealth. But I thought what the hell, just because old Prissy passed out at her first public event, in front of her bosses, their bosses, every last one of her colleagues and the public, didn't mean she'd be home by Christmas. Or they'd send her home Monday.

What Prissy needed was to disappear. Get out from under the glare of the limelight. I moved to her side, excusing myself with the longstocking woman, who had also been drinking the punch, or had lost the ability to focus. "Come along there, Miss Johnson," I said. "Let's get you a little fresh air. Stuffy in here. I'm sure you're not used to this tropical weather and all this fresh fruit punch."

Prissy said, "Mmmm."

"Okay," I told her. "Upsy daisy." I put my back into it but she was dead weight, passed out drunk. "Well. Looks like we need a little hand here."

Four guys volunteered to help me. I only wanted one. We each took a limb and hoisted her from the couch. The longstocking woman looked on in bleary condescension. We marched away, the odd man stumbling alongside hugging the drinks. Immediately behind me my wife said, "What in the hell do you boys think you're doing?"

My wife Patricia is one of those women who spends way too much time looking out for other women. "We need to move her," I explained.

"Where?"

"To bed."

"Like hell."

We were now making a scene. "Fine," I said. "We'll just dump her on the floor."

She isn't a bad person, my wife, she just believes that all men are up to something evil and she's the police. "Follow me," she ordered. "We are not using Dale Sterling's bedroom and she will not need her clothes removed for any reason."

One of the drunks helping me said, "We gotta make her comfortable."

There's always one idiot. "Shut up," I told him. I couldn't even see who it was, I had a foot.

We laid Prissy out in a guest bedroom. Placed her on her back, folded her hands corpse-like across her abdomen, and started for the door. "Just a minute," my wife said. She lined us up. "No one comes back in here. Ever. Do you understand me?"

"What if she pukes?" the drunk asked. "Sucks it back into her lungs. Somebody ought to watch her."

"Let her die," Patricia told him. "Or you die."

Drunks prefer clear choices, and they all filed out except me. "There's something to what he says," I said.

"I'll keep an eye on her. Poor thing. Imagine how embarrassed she'll be in the morning when all this comes back to her and she realizes what a mess she's made." Patricia's eyes flitted around the room. "Who gave her all that booze to drink?"

"Not me," I said. "She was drinking the punch."

"That you warned me about?"

"Yes."

"Why didn't you warn her?"

"Made a bet."

She pushed me ahead through the door, hard. "I hope you lose."

The party wore on and Patricia made frequent trips to Prissy's room. Twice she claimed to have found men in there. Just talking to her, they said. Shortly after midnight the guaguita was going to make its first run and take the early-to-bedders home. Patricia came and got me. "We'll get her on the bus and home for a good night's rest," she said. "Maybe she won't be quite so hung over in the morning. It'll all be forgotten."

"Okay," I said. "I'll get somebody to help me."

"No. You carry her yourself."

"She weighs a ton."

"Put her over your shoulder. You're a man aren't you?"

She was a long woman, draped across my right shoulder it was like carrying a gutted deer. I'd tried to wake her first, just in case she could stagger out to the bus on her own, but she was unconscious and in what seemed a hypnotic state, except she wasn't obedient at all. Filiberto slid open the side door to the minibus, openly grinning at the limp form like a guy who'd just been given the keys to the harem boudoir.

"Wait!" my wife said.

Filiberto, another idiot.

"Where is she staying?" Patricia demanded.

"Miz Russell's," Filiberto answered.

Ms. Deborah K. Russell of the U.S. Embassy was Vice President of the School Board. She was also very rich, very generous, and not the kind of a woman you wanted for an enemy.

"We know where Russells live," she told Filiberto. "We'll take her."

Filiberto was crestfallen and I could see he blamed me for not controlling my wife – a failing of which Latino men never tire of pointing out to American men. "Just shut up," I told him. "Some nights a guy feels like two women, even if he has to carry one."

"Put her in the car," Patricia ordered. Our car was three blocks along the street.

I tucked her in the backseat gently. Her head lolled to the side. She said "Mmmm."

Ms. Russell lived in Naco, an exclusive neighborhood with its own strip mall and theaters. The house was very large and well staffed so we decided on a side door. Servants would admit us and poor Prissy could be put to bed without arousing the owners.

Patricia led the way along a stone path through the bougainvillea to an iron gate probably used for deliveries. A hike from where I'd parked the car.

"Hurry up," I said. "She's heavy."

"It's dark. I'm wearing heels."

The gate was locked. She rattled it and we waited.

"I can't stand here like this all night," I said. "Go around front."

She rattled the gate again. "Just wait. She can't be that heavy."

Prissy's body was warm. I'd positioned her on my shoulder so neither her rib cage or pelvic bones cut into my clavicle. There was a certain intimacy in our joining. She seemed content and I was more comfortable with the burden now than before, like a pack you've carried until it has a familiar weight and feel. She didn't stir or moan. She was truly dead weight and her sandals were in the lower front pockets of my cream guayabera.

"Nobody's coming," I said.

We went around front. "They're going to know," Patricia predicted as she lifted the knocker.

"Everybody knows anyway. It'll blow over."

We waited. Patricia knocked repeatedly, louder and louder. If there'd been any close neighbors we'd have awakened them too.

"There's nobody here," Patricia said.

"Doesn't make sense."

"Unless the higher-ups have another party to go to same as us," she said. "Might've given the servants the night off."

"Check Prissy's pockets for a key. They'd give her a key then."

"She doesn't have pockets," Patricia said. "She's barely got a dress. I'll get her purse. It's in the car."

"She's not light, you know."

"Oh, calm down. You're not walking, you're just holding her. I'll be right back."

Prissy and I stood there in the darkness of the luxurious front portico. It looked pink in the dark. The pillars and railings white and freshly painted. There was no light inside.

No key either as it turned out.

"Now what?" I asked. "It's almost one o'clock."

"I know, and I promised Joy I'd help her make a few things at her party too. We were supposed to be at their house early."

"It's a drive yet," I said. "We could just take her with us, I guess. Chances are she'll come to before long."

Patricia nodded. "Makes sense. Let's hurry."

We arrived at the Ferris apartment at about one-thirty in the morning. The party was noisy and I had to park more than a block away. Well, it couldn't be helped. I got out and started up the street.

"Where are you going?" Patricia asked.

"Where do you think?"

"Without Prissy?"

"She's fine where she is."

"Don't be silly. Pick her up."

"Patricia. Bill and Joy live on the third floor. I'm not carrying her up three flights of stairs, I don't care what you say. I locked the car. She'll be just fine. If she wakes up she'll hear the music and come on up."

It was the second floor that nearly did me in, not the first or third. Patricia knocked but I had to nearly kick the door in before anyone answered, and then it was some guy I'd never seen before. He hollered to Joy, "Hey! There's some people here with a corpse."

"No!" someone else shouted. "It's Prissy. You brought Prissy. Oh, where should we put her?"

We tried the couch first but her head lolled. We tried a chair with a hassock but her dress was too slick and she slipped onto the floor. Finally I carried her to the spare bedroom and Patricia got promises from several other women to help act as lookouts.

Our host, Bill Ferris, taught algebra and drank to excess. Otherwise I never saw him do anything useful. Most of the time he was drunk before a party got started. Once we walked in early someplace and he was actually lying on the floor under the bar singing a filthy limerick. Everybody loved him. He was an ugly man and he said to me, "Hey, Mosby. You're sweating."

"What do you expect? I carried Prissy up here. Why don't you live on the ground floor?"

"We like the breeze. Did you get a drink? Hey, who is this woman?"

"New hire."

"Nice build on her."

"You haven't been in the bedroom?"

"Yeah," he said, sniggering. "But your wife caught me."

The Ferris party went on until about 4:30 or 5 o'clock, and most everyone was ready for breakfast somewhere so we could watch the sun come up over the ocean. Prissy had been left pretty much alone, although people who hadn't attended the other party were all taken in to see her. They seemed to fall in love with her, like a new puppy. Someone had given her a conch shell to hold.

Patricia and I decided to head home and get Prissy to bed. I wasn't looking forward to carrying her down the stairs again but by this

time it was a matter of pride to me that the burden was mine alone.
We started out the door and someone asked, "Where you going with
Prissy? You're coming down to breakfast, right?"

"No," Patricia said. "We've got to get her home."

"Oh, no! It's not a party without Prissy. Where we go, she goes."

I adjusted her weight on my shoulder. "Listen, I can't keep
carrying this girl around the city all night."

"Just to Karin's," a woman said. "We'll take tables right by the
curb and you can leave her in the car. Roll the window down. She'll
be a few feet away. Just so she's with us."

They all joined in then and we were too tired to argue. Anyway, I
was hungry. I'd missed dinner and most of the snacks were stale. So
Prissy went to breakfast.

The sun slid up over the airport peninsula and sprayed a mint
green light on the sea. I sat where I could watch Prissy inside the
backseat. I'd found an old blanket in the trunk and folded it under
her head, which rested on the open window. Her fine hair had
loosened from the careful bun she'd made of it and the morning
breezes brushed it in wisps across her face. I sipped the strong bitter
coffee and thought how I'd never spoken a word to Pricilla Johnson,
but in some ways knew more about her than almost anyone. I knew
what it was like to hold her, to pick her up and lie her down, to
feel her warm stomach against my shoulder, and I knew the gentle
rhythm of her breathing.

Patricia was busy talking to Joy about her favorite subject, which
is sunbathing, and it seemed that I was alone with Prissy then, at
sunrise. The pair of us by the sea, ten feet apart. She wasn't heavily
perfumed but I recalled her scent, citrus oil of some kind. I didn't
think she'd dressed provocatively, either. Somebody probably told
her at the last minute it was a dress-up and she'd gone for a dress, or
borrowed one that didn't fit.

I watched the sun rotate from the sea to cast a warming, blonde
light on her face. I'd never seen her in true light, and got up and

strolled across the sidewalk. The soft yellow of early morning lit the fine hairs on her cheek and chin. I bent over and kissed her.

Straightening up, my gaze followed the Malecón westward to where I'd passed Trujillo's last stand that morning, and the very same fear, followed by a sense of well-being, settled into my heart and I thought it odd that violent death and foolish innocence should elicit the same emotion.

When I got back to the table Patricia was staring but didn't say anything.

"She looked so lonely there," I explained.

Patricia nodded and smiled at me.

"Further along here is where they killed Trujillo," I said.

"I know," she answered. "A lot happens here."

Denise

From a bluff where I stood on the North Shore, a breeze
blew fresh and chilly across the gray chop of the great lake. On
the horizon, chubby gray clouds stampeded before the wind,
underbellies ripped away, dragging the dull water. I wrapped both
hands around a steaming cup of coffee, wringing the last drops of
warmth between noisy gulps. Another dismal stretch of weather
and I was short staffed again, which meant four, maybe six hours in
42-degree water.

"It'll be a bitch out there today," a voice said at my elbow.
"Especially for that lot." It was Paul, my divemaster, pointing out
four young people moving across from the line of cabins toward
a low ridge that ran parallel to the water. One swung a bottle
of whiskey by its neck. "They've been at it all night," he said,
disapproval heavy in his voice.

Only two of the four would be diving, and I picked them out from
the group. Both girls, young, college age. I supposed the other two
were boyfriends, along to watch. The girls stood taller then the
boys and wore their hair shorter, highlighted with sharp colors of

green and pink. All four were attired in black leather outfits, like those worn then by rock singers. One boy's thin feminine wrist was encircled by a menacing black leather bracelet embedded with sharp silver spikes.

I smiled at Paul. "Frightening, aren't they?"

"Laugh if you like," he said. "Your life's on the line down there when they panic."

"They're just kids showing off," I said, to reassure myself. "Besides, they made it this far."

"Warm swimming pool is one thing. Forty-degree water and white caps are something else." Paul gave me a hard look, then grinned and crossed his eyes in that goofy way he had. "But you're the instructor. I just do what I'm told." And with that he strolled off in the direction of his cabin.

I remained awhile, wondering if after all he hadn't been right. Conditions were lousy, especially for a training dive. But then Lake Superior conditions were always lousy. Either too cold, or too hot, or too windy or the underwater visibility was too low. If you waited for good conditions the job never got done.

The coffee in the bottom of my cup had gone cold. I flipped it out onto the slick grass and hiked back to assemble my equipment. It started to rain - methodical, soaking. The weather would just have to do, that's all.

By half past nine that morning I was watching the fluorescent red tip of Paul's snorkel shrink ever smaller as he made his way out from shore towing the float and flag behind him. I wondered if he felt as lonely as he looked - tossing, visible intermittently between the silver steel waves. I turned to the small group of shivering students and smiled bravely.

"It's not as bad as it looks," I said. "Swim steadily. Pace yourselves to avoid exhaustion. I'll be with you all the way."

They absorbed the initial cold water shock and settled down to a comfortable pace. All six were good swimmers, and we had plowed our way nearly half the distance to the float before one of them began to tire noticeably and fall behind. I moved closer. Her pace began to slow even more. I slid in next to her, very close, but she gave no indication she'd seen me. She labored for each breath and I listened to the air rush in and out of her snorkel like a sucking drain. The transparent tube was coated inside with foaming saliva and each gasping breath came faster than the last.

"Stop!" I said.

She swam on.

Another few strokes would push her over the edge. Her perceptions narrowing, focused inward. Soon she'd hyperventilate and panic.

I swam forward and used my body to block her path. Her head came up.

"Inflate your BC," I commanded. "Rest."

She fumbled for the mechanical inflator attached to the buoyancy control device. I listened to the reassuring sound of low pressure air rushing through the valve and into the BC. The orange jacket ballooned to twice its size and gently rolled her face up. Only then did she spit the snorkel from her mouth and remove her mask.

She gasped for air and warm tears pumped from her eyes. "I can't," she sobbed. "I can't do it." Her head rolled toward me. "I'm sorry."

"Rest," I said. "What's your name?"

"Denise."

"Take it easy, Denise. You'll feel better when your breathing slows down."

"I'm so scared," she cried. "Stay with me?"

"As long as you want," I promised. "The others will catch up to Paul. No hurry."

She rested then, spread-eagled on top of the water, crying.

The frigid lake washed over us in choppy waves that seemed to come from two directions. Intermittently she gasped for air.

There wasn't anything for me to do but watch her and offer encouragement. When her strength returned she'd either continue the dive, or quit and go home. I'd take it personally if she quit. I always did. It was my failure too, even though she was just one of hundreds to take classes that summer and her pool and classroom were done with another instructor. But I hate losing, and the longer we waited tossing on the surface, the worse our chances. Too much time to think. I wanted to scream for her to roll over and swim. Pound her fins against the water. Butt her head into the waves. Push on.

I said none of those things, only watched, until finally her head came up and she looked at me. "Are you mad at me?"

"Don't be stupid."

The crying stopped but her face was still wet with tears and lake water. "I'm strong," she said, "and tall for a girl."

"Size doesn't go for much out here."

She seemed to think that over. "What now?" she asked.

"You decide."

That's the moment. I'd seen it many times. People try to manage their lives so they never face such a time, not clearly anyway, and of those who do face it, most turn aside. Some go on in spite of their fear. It's fine that it's an exact moment, an identifiable one, though I've never decided how many people recognize that. Denise did, I think. I watched her deciding.

"I want to do it."

"Best choice you ever made," I said, and we swam on.

Denise turned twenty-one that summer. But I saw little of her. Like many college students who took scuba - for a lark or to earn PE credit - she completed the requirements and disappeared. I soon forgot her.

Months passed, a year, and it was summer again. Denise returned. She had changed.

The short, punk hairstyle remained, but more subdued and

chestnut brown from the roots. The multiple earrings, once dangling and twisting against each another, were replaced by less distracting choices. Her clothing too, was softer. The face was the same - small, impish, smooth-skinned around a large elfin nose. Though she was just below my height, her long neck seemed to stretch higher, her face at the end of it, a happy mask.

But the change was more than superficial. That summer Denise completed every continuing education course our association offered and spent a good deal of money purchasing the scuba equipment she'd need to make her living as a scuba instructor. I watched in awe as she attacked one course after the next without complaint or return of her previous doubt.

Most of these courses were given by other instructors and it wasn't until August that I taught her Rescue Class. I'd learned something about her by then. I knew she was an art major, and one of her watercolors hung in my dive shop, a school of tropical fish she had never seen, except in photographs. They were drawn too wide, I'd decided, but I liked them.

The Rescue Class was taught at Big Fish Lake. Its packed sand extended from shore to a depth of eight or ten feet. Rescue is mostly practice. Teams work in twos, charging the water, stripping and donning equipment as swiftly as it can be done. It's physical, fast, hard training. Repetition converts theory into the automatic, reflexive skill necessary to save a life.

Denise's class was mostly male, as classes were then. She was a big girl but I paired her with the smallest of the men, a Bulgarian who bragged he'd escaped Communism. Trained as an instructor by the Russian military, he wanted to replace his invalid Russian certification with an international one. He resented the courses he was forced to take. They were nothing, he said, compared to what the Soviets had put him through. He complained about the money he was wasting to repeat something he'd already learned.

I paired him with Denise because of his size and my suspicion that he was full of hot air. She was a good head taller, appeared stronger, and had longer legs. With a pair of Jet Fins on her feet, few divers in the water could keep abreast of Denise, including me. The Bulgarian student had told me there weren't any female divers in Eastern Europe and suggested we might be effeminate, allowing such things here. This rankled me more because it threatened my own manhood I suppose, then the obvious slur toward the opposite sex, but I chose Denise as my equalizer. "Isn't hurting you, is she?" I'd say later. I had faith in her by then, you see.

Successful scuba instructors, like winning coaches, watch and repeat. They watch each individual's performance, examine it in detail, and order it repeated until weaknesses are beaten into strengths. They call it practice, but it's rote learning; the only sure route to success at anything that requires instant response.

To rescue someone in the water, the first problem is the rescuer, who faces greater risk then the victim. Panicked victims can climb onto the heads of their rescuers and drown them. This danger must be anticipated and the response perfected by practice. By mid-afternoon Denise was tired of Eastern Europe. She took me aside. "I want a new partner," she demanded. "A new buddy. This guy is rough. He's hurting me."

"In a real rescue, that might happen," I said.

"This is class."

"I know. You seem to be handling him okay."

"He's hurting me."

There was a flaming scrape on her neck, a small cut on one finger. "You just carried him to shore," I said.

"He tightened up and tried to wiggle out of the carry. Who would do that? He's strong. Give him to one of the guys."

"Okay," I said. "Guess he was right about girls in diving."

I was still smoking in those days and Denise reached out with damp fingers, pulled the cigarette from my mouth and crushed it.

"Smoking sucks," she said and leaned almost to my nose. "What are we trying to prove?"

"Nothing," I lied. "We're just trying to be the best damn rescuers we can possibly be. Isn't that what you hoped for when you signed up for this class? Don't you want the confidence that comes knowing you can handle yourself in any situation?"

We stood like that longer than was comfortable but I'd learned Denise didn't have any meanness in her, and without warning the impish smile returned. She shrugged and said, "Sweet Jesus. He's going to kill me."

He tried.

The most dangerous rescue isn't underwater but on the surface. Underwater rescues are decided in seconds, and failure can turn them into body recoveries. On the surface there's a chance to save a life only if the rescuer overcomes the panicked victim. I'd cautioned the "victims" against superhuman resistance that might turn practice into a dangerous reality. They were to resist, but not clobber their rescuers. "Don't bully anybody," I warned, staring pointedly at the Bulgarian.

His malevolent smile held fixed, unwavering.

I remained on shore, gear piled ready beside me, binoculars on my chest. When I called the four teams of two into action, the victims a hundred yards from shore began to panic, waving their arms, shouting and splashing. The rescuers donned complete scuba and swam for them on the surface using snorkel.

Through the glasses I saw the Bulgarian's smirk. His arms barely moved up and down in a poor performance of a panicked diver and beneath the surface he pumped his legs like a stallion at the gate. Denise moved swiftly, closing the distance. The tip of her snorkel hissed air and light silver spray.

She halted beyond his reach. "Inflate your BC!" I heard her bellow.

He remained as before. Strangely quiet. Unresponsive.

"Inflate your BC!"

She moved closer.

"Watch it," I whispered. "Watch it!"

The water churned. His legs drove his body forward and he had her round the neck, pressing her head underwater and into his chest, knees pounding her stomach and breasts.

Victims were required to tread water without aid of BC inflation. No buoyancy. Each wore a twenty pound lead weight belt. There existed a very real danger in this. Not even the strongest swimmer can tread water long with that much negative buoyancy.

Denise had been talking to her victim and had neither snorkel or regulator mouthpiece. Crushed against his chest she was starved for air, destined to become the victim within seconds. Glasses pressed to my eyes, she seemed in imminent danger. I thought of calling a halt, but would the Bulgarian listen? Would he respond or wait until she was defeated and show his superiority by rescuing the rescuer?

I saw Denise's hand recover her regulator and wedge it into her mouth. With the other hand she deflated her own BC and began to sink, forcing the Bulgarian to support her weight and his own. This realization came late to him; arms and legs weary from the pounding he'd given her. Denise's head passed beneath the water and she tripped the quick release on his weight belt as she went by so he couldn't descend and follow her.

A moment later she rose behind him out of reach, and holding his tank to keep him facing away, she inflated his BC, ignoring his helpless flailing arms and towed him toward shore.

"Nicely done," I said as she ground his tank into the sand.

She tried a smile but her lower lip was split and bleeding. "Ouch," she complained to me.

The Bulgarian was quiet.

"In a minute," I said, "after your victim has had time to rest, it'll be your turn," I told her. "Be sure and give him the same amount of realism he gave you."

Somewhere in there Denise and I became friends. Maybe not the kind you tell your secrets to, but colleague conspirators, planning her adventures, recalling mine. "I'm going to become a scuba instructor," she told me once again, "and spend my life at sea traveling the Caribbean Islands." I respected her determination and understood the dream. And so in some ways, we were even closer than friends.

In late September she qualified for an instructor course and we commented on the coincidence of me teaching her first and last scuba course. She was an exceptionally bright student and left nothing to chance as she learned the teaching methods for classroom, pool, and open water. She graduated at the top of her class.

"I'll miss you," she said on our last day. "You're in my logbook but I wrote *curmudgeon* behind your name that day in Rescue Class you made me drag that Bulgarian soldier out of the water. He was rough with me and I don't care if you did it to make me tough or what, I'm still mad at you. I *am*. Curmudgeon." She hugged me, almost reaching down to do it, and I saw tears and felt very curmudgeonly indeed.

The new equipment I'd sold her a short time before was worn now as she packed it up to begin her adventure. Our repair department had serviced her regulator and she was buying spare fin and mask straps. "What will you do?" I asked. "Where will you go?"

"Work," she said. "Start in Florida, I think. Got a few hundred saved up."

"You can't just say you're going off to Florida to *work* when you don't have a job. Anyway, where are you going in Florida?"

"By the water."

"Great plan." I took her hand. "Listen, try Palm Beach. I know charter boat people there. Probably not hiring, but it's a place to start. I go down in the winter too."

She favored me with a lopsided grin. "I grew up on the farm picking potatoes," she said. "I know hard work and I don't think you can go anywhere and not find a job if you know hard work."

I didn't see her the rest of that year nor did I hear anything from the people I'd put her in touch with in Palm Beach, but early the following year I took a group of divers to Singer Island near West Palm and there I found Denise working in a tourist shop selling T-shirts and faded sea shells. Sand littered the sidewalk, shining in the heat and a buzzer sounded when I opened the door. We hugged in a dozen convex shoplifting mirrors and I thought she looked thin.

"Do you have any idea the markup on this junk?" she whispered. "Astronomical! Even the dive shops down here make more selling T-shirts then scuba gear. I'm not kidding. Sometimes I sell a hundred smiley-faces a day. The ones with the bullet holes in their heads are best though."

I wasn't fooled. "Unless they give you a big commission, you're earning minimum wage like everybody else on this beach. How can you afford to live?"

"We're not going to my place for dinner," she said, grinning. "It's a dump. But, they let me go along on the dive boat now for free, if I work."

"You're working for free?"

"For awhile. Until they see how good I am."

"You're a fully certified instructor."

"Without experience and from the Midwest," she finished. "They think we only know mud holes and shallow dives."

"Come home," I said. "I'm short an instructor for the summer."

She shook her head. "Thanks, but this is my thing." She led me behind a large sign - 50% OFF! "I never had a goal, you know? Just this vague artistic *deal* I borrowed from college Profs. Phony crap. That first day in the water, remember? So cold. My body was numb but my mind raced a million miles an hour. My life flickering by and I asked *What now*? and you said, 'You decide.' Remember that day? That was the moment I took charge." She shrugged at the rumpled T-shirt piles. "It may not seem like it to you, but I *am* in charge. People don't know it yet, that's all."

On my next trip to Florida she was gone. Off working on one of the local boats I was told. Then I lost track of her and rumor had it she left Florida. It wasn't the first time I'd seen it happen in diving. People swallowed up in a world-wide system of boats, resorts, and shops - young Americans, Australians, Canadians, Britons, Europeans - drifting from place to place working for little more than their living and the chance to dive the best sites, taste something of the world. You encountered them on the charter boats; lean and tan, earringed and braceleted, bleached and smiling. I never envied them.

Another year slipped by and I settled into my 40s, squawking. In February our charter flight landed on Grand Cayman fifteen minutes ahead of schedule and as I dashed from customs in search of the bus, Denise flung her arms around my neck.

"It's you," I said. "How'd you know I was on this plane?"

"I didn't," she said sheepishly. "Those are my parents coming behind you."

Later we had a drink at one of the waterfront bars. She'd been in Cayman almost since I'd lost track of her and was leaving within the next few months. "Finally," she said, "I'm there."

"Where?"

"This time I'm going to sea. No more day boats - same old reef, same dive briefing, same fish. I know their names for crying out loud! Finally got a live-aboard: *Undersea Dreamer*. At sea every day. We spend a week or two with the divers so there's time to get to know them. Diving's bad, we haul anchor and move. She's nearly 160-feet long and I get my own cabin. Can you believe it? I mean it's all really happening. Can I dive with you tomorrow? I want to put you in my logbook again."

"Sure. Be a privilege," I said. "After all, how often do I get to dive with such an old salt?"

She stuck her tongue out.

That next afternoon I marveled at her effortlessness, the quiet assurance of this gangly Minnesota girl moving through the sea with the grace of a porpoise. Beside her I felt clumsy, last year's model. Could this truly be the same girl I'd seen when I stood with Paul on a hill overlooking the frigid waters of Lake Superior, watching her amble along with some kid swinging a bottle of whiskey? In answer, bubbles streamed in a steady, controlled exhalation from the exhaust ports of her regulator and the scuffed Jet Fins I'd sold her long ago seemed grafted to her feet as she slipped through the water, across the face of the reef, and down along the warm sand channel toward the blue depths.

My pride followed, a stain of envy too. The student had surpassed the teacher, so I asserted myself and assumed the lead, taking us deeper into the channel where I spotted a large opening in the reef, and leaning left, I kicked into the dim light of a cave. She trailed along behind.

The cave was larger than it appeared from outside and lit by several round skylight holes, shafts of pale light flickering on the sand. Above, a dozen Blue Chromis spun like living neon in endless circles that brought me to my knees. Denise settled beside me, fascinated. I realized then that she had no idea why I'd overtaken her and led us here. A moment later, she plucked the thin glove from her left hand and interlocked her fingers with mine. An unconditional gesture of simple friendship, maybe even thanks.

We sat there side by side for awhile, and it calmed me. Her eyes behind the faceplate were alive, bright as when she first shared her youthful fancy. We swam on further inside the cave then, into smaller rooms, until we'd lost most of the light from the large mouth and settled for what filtered from cracks and fissures in the rock. Our fins stirred the sand and left a dust in the shafted light as might be disturbed in an attic room, and I led on deeper and deeper into the labyrinth.

The cave ended in a sharp wall of gray bumpy rock, but beyond, a small tunnel opened to the sea again. It was just large enough for us to traverse in single file and I entered without hesitation. Denise followed.

The floor of the tunnel was warm sand. The roof, rugged limestone. We were forced to avoid an increasing forest of stalactites, extending at times almost to the sand. The ocean had once been much lower and the cave above water. My movements became erratic as I twisted to avoid catching a regulator or high pressure hose on the jagged rock and coral. My tank clanged and finning room was restricted. I tried to move without kicking my legs. Craning my neck I saw Denise following at a safe distance. Her eyes wide behind the safety plate.

We worked into the narrowing passage toward the aquamarine light of our exit. Schools of French Grunts and the ever-present Squirrel fish moved across the opening and it seemed another few kick cycles would bring us out among them. Instead, my tank clanged. Sharp chips of rock struck my back and when I tried to kick free a shortened stalactite pressed the steel tank against my spine and pinned me hard to the sand.

This critical threat amused me at first. Conceit had driven me beyond the limits of sound judgment just when we were low on air. Foolishness, I thought, but if I'm lucky it won't kill me. I dug the heels of my hands into the sand and pushed back hard. The stalactite held fast, a point of force for the tons of rock above. I was fastened to the bottom of the tunnel. In a few minutes I'd be out of air. Three feet away, in the freedom of the open sea, a grouper paused to give me the eye and swim on. A warm dazzling sea, seducer of the experienced as well as the novice. The sea is enemy and friend, responding to nothing but its own moods, granting ecstasy or terror with capricious indifference.

Denise pulled herself along the back of my legs and struck my tank with something. The metallic banging scattered the fish. She struck again. I shook my head. She'd never loosen the stalactite by hitting the tank. She struck again. She was using a knife I decided, and held my hand up, wagging a finger for her to stop. I thought maybe she couldn't see the stalactite in the disturbed water. Then I felt her hand grasp my waistband strap and jerk at it.

Take the tank off. That's what she wanted. I clawed the sand with my fingers and dug a hole deep enough to slip the quick release, then another to pinch the chest strap. With some struggling and worming I had it off and beside me. I drew it up and turned it, then pushed the tank ahead as I squirmed free and out into open water. A minute later I was on the surface.

Denise took her time and worked back down and out the larger mouth of the cave. When she joined me on the surface neither of us spoke.

She offered no help as I slipped back into the BC and clicked the straps.

"Close," I said.

She reached over and patted my belly. "Wouldn't hurt you to push back from the table now and then."

Before long, middle-age loomed large behind the usual mountains of regret. Forties. I was less sure of things. Two years, then three passed, and once again I'd lost track of Denise and wondered from time to time, whatever happened to that girl? Did she find what she was searching for? Answers beneath the waves? I hadn't found them there.

It wasn't formaldehyde or embalming fluid but the fragrance of too many flowers that choked me in the chapel. Their visual splendor defeated by an unrelenting attack on the nose. I inhaled shallow breathes at forced intervals.

The casket was closed - we all knew it would be - and covered with photographs. I examined each of them closely, though I'd seen many before, and some I'd taken. There were other items too. Her scuba equipment, what little was recovered, and smaller things that must've been left in her dive bag that day - an underwater flashlight, a rusty knife, lobster gauge. At the head of the casket was a small table filled with logbooks and other writings. A crowd gathered there. On the walls, her watercolors.

I'd been asked to give a eulogy the following afternoon at the funeral, but begged off. I was beginning a new instructor class. Looking back on it, my motives to teach weren't much different than a mother driven to pregnancy after a stillborn. Life renewed. Faith restored. I wanted to see another Denise walking out the door confident, swaggering with youth and promise. I had nothing to say about her that could be embraced by death. Accidents are sad death. Unlike illness or old age, they're preventable, so we grasp at the notion that we can stop them all. Futile thoughts, and no salve for our sorrow, so I did what people do - I grieved for her.

In the months following Denise's death, her accident became controversial. It was freakish to begin with. Aboard *Undersea Dreamer* not far from the Caribbean island of St. Martin, part of the Lesser Antilles, Denise was supervising divers at the stern when a safety rope attached to an orange float ball became entangled in the vessel's propeller. This posed no threat since *Undersea Dreamer* was not underway and there was plenty of time to remove the rope before departure. The boat's captain however, could not see the stern from the pilothouse and depended on messages relayed to him as to how work was progressing.

Denise entered the water once all divers were back onboard and attempted to untangle the propeller. Unsuccessful in her first attempt, she came back aboard to find a pry tool. When the captain called down from the pilothouse to ask if the prop was clear and Denise safely back aboard, a crewman saw her and said yes.

Meanwhile, Denise went back into the water to finish the job. Her head and upper body were between the propeller blades when the captain engaged the engine. Though she died instantly, it was several moments before anyone realized what happened.

Ignored by "respectable" media, the tragedy attracted tabloid television. In her grief, Denise's mother insisted I be interviewed and grudgingly I agreed. After a few weeks, two boys arrived in a rented Lincoln and scratched my furniture with their "television equipment," explaining how they'd ask questions and later the show's host would be dubbed in so it would appear she'd actually asked them herself. Questions which were not questions but provocations designed to illicit dishonest or speculative responses. I was being asked to participate in a pre-arranged script, a drama of misfortune to entertain the tabloid TV audience of the simple-minded who thrive on the misery of others.

I gave truthful answers. They especially disliked the one: "I don't know, I wasn't there." This frustrated the teenagers, who'd urged me to be emotional, allow a tear down my cheek. I fumbled the repeat questions, smiled at the camera. When the segment finally aired, not one second of my interview made the cut.

Who understood that I didn't empathize with Denise, but with her captain? The man who killed her. It was his hand on the throttle and he literally took her life in an instant, doing nothing more than what was to him a daily chore. That moment in his life would haunt him forever, a fog that never blew clear. Living with a crippled faith in himself. Could he trust his own judgment as before? The rest, the uncertainty, the disquieted heart, only death might free.

And I shared his heartache too. My mind flew back to the freezing waters of Lake Superior. My hand was on the throttle that day. I could've sent her to shore and very likely changed the course of her life. I might've saved her, saved her captain, her family. Saved myself from years of wondering, doubting, finding fault.

Did Denise calculate the cost of her youthful dreams? I don't know, but she died in the midst of her aspirations, unlike many of us who die later in the midst of our illusions. She was my hero for that. From the table near her casket that funeral day, I'd picked up a logbook and thumbed it. The pages were coated with a water resistant gloss, but even so, some of the writing was smudged. Logbooks recording a life. Notes on water temperature and clarity, times and depths and air consumption. Breaths consumed. Inhale, exhale. Exhale one final time. My name was written there, on the line entitled Dive Buddy - Curmudgeon.

Jimmy Olsen

Sea Salt

Martha Ebanks said "Humph," a frequent expression, especially when she glanced out the open window and caught sight of the boy carrying the white sack. She said "humph" closed-mouthed and louder than anyone on the cay, and the island too. The boy heard it, and smiled.

The back door was ajar and he called from outside, "It's me - Cangrejo de duna!"

"Yes, Sand Crab. Bring the bag. Old man's lunch is ready. Take it. When you come back I give you a haircut. You look like your mother."

"Fat from your rice, beans, platano and butter? I'm thin," he teased, patting his stomach. "Her skin was dark as yours, I'm light. Her hair down on her shoulders, mine is not."

She waited until he crossed the small kitchen. "I miss her little Cangrejo." She stroked him. "I talk to her sometimes, when I'm alone. After I buried her I couldn't imagine living in this wasteland another day. This luna duna! This salt flat."

"But here we are, Grana."

"Yes," she said. "But things are changing, even here."

"The hotel."

"The hotel."

"The old man doesn't want it."

"I care what an old man wants? Humph! He has nothing to say about it. He's not the government. An employee of the salt company, and the salt company is nothing compared to the tourist companies that build hotels and buy the diving boats and make a restaurant."

The boy remained silent. Like the old man, he hated the idea of the hotel. A thing to be feared like invasion by a desperate foreign army, robbing them of the cay forever. Tourist armies, tall buildings towering above them, splintering the sunsets. He loved the naked cay, the low sheds, bedraggled palms, salt piles, the evaporation dams and crystallization pans. These were natural and didn't rob sea or sky of its open, boundless space. At a glance Salt Cay was nothing, a desolate industrial maze, but close up it was alive with everything that made life mysterious.

"I go now," he said. "Maybe there is Coca Cola?"

"No. The Coca has been gone for days. Why do you ask me?" She filled his sack with metal pots and pans, lids secured with duct tape. "The rice is still warm. Squid in blue sauce that you like. When the hotel is finished, then there will be Coca Cola."

"I won't want it then."

"You are too young to be so set in your ways," she said and drew him close. "It's because you spend all your time with old ones. You should be in school."

"I will make salt."

She pressed his head between her ample breasts and kissed his hair. "Go to your sea salt and your salt man. Bring some conch in for supper and tell old Simon that Perdomo was here with some grouper and fresh vegetables from the island, so it's a good night for him to come in. Remind him he has not paid me this month and he should bring more than just his appetite."

The Ebanks boy wiggled free of her. "He is close with his money, that old man."

"He has little enough of it," she said and patted his cheek. "You will have to carry water tonight, too."

A cactus fence with a wooden gate enclosed the sand yard and the boy kicked it open as he swung the sack smoothly over his shoulder and walked away. The pans made a soft rattle and were warm against his thin shirt. The sun was high and the sand hot.

Medoro Ebanks, boy of twelve, with the light brown eyes of his mulatto father who he'd never seen, drew in a deep, moist breath of air and smelled the salt and smiled. His gaze swept the cay - sand below, sky above - like a loggerhead adrift in the deep blue, then another time, as now, motionless and rigid in the sun.

Medo followed the conch path a long distance to the first evaporation dam and climbed onto the lip that held the seawater and the weirs. The height was not great but the cay was flat and any elevation provided a vista. Simon was working at the pans, drawing off the bitterns and making ready for the salt harvest now before the storm season. The old man claimed he could dip his finger and taste the water and know if it was ready for draining. Medo wondered if he was down inside, near the pan floor, where he couldn't see him.

Sometimes the old man worked among the line of abandoned slave cabins, whitewashing and cleaning them like shrines. He slept there on nights Grana Ebanks drank rum; crawled inside to nap sometimes after his lunch. A white man who drove the bulldozer at harvest once asked Medo, "Why are there so many dog houses?" The boy laughed and told him they were slave huts. The man had studied them then and said finally, "They must've been small people." Medo told him, "No. They were crowded people." The huts were no larger than bread ovens.

Medo saw no movement among the huts. Simon's white head and shirt camouflaged him in the salt. The clear seawater in the pans seemed white too, a brackish brine increasing in salt content daily as the water evaporated. Outside the area of dams, pans and canals, the sea was at peace, a great salt lake, stealing blue from the mid-day sky to cover its bare back.

The boy's trained eyes spotted the dull flash of a shovel in the light. White head bobbing, the old man cleared a storm canal. He worked hardest before lunch and supper, as if finishing a race. Medo did not call out but loped along the dams, jumping weirs, jogging the connecting roadways that zigzagged across acres of evaporating seawater, an industrial no man's land that to Medo was an empty battlefield of mysterious delight.

"I'm here," he said at last.

The old man shoveled on - scraping, tossing - without acknowledging the boy. His back bent to the sun, shoulders rounded, worn by the work. The white shirt hung on him, stark against the sable skin of his muscular forearms and knotted hands. He was a beautiful old man.

"Blue squid," the boy said. "Rice and goat's milk."

Simon pushed the shovel into the sand and pressed one fist into the small of his back. "Purple," he said. "It's not blue. It's purple."

Medo smiled. "Tastes the same."

The old man climbed from the canal and they walked together along the road between the evaporating water to the shade of a far shed.

"Is she going to take you to the island?" Simon asked. "When the hotel in finished?"

"The hotel is like a dream for her." He watched the sky, empty of birds. "It's like a dream of Heaven."

Simon nodded. "A dream of Heaven, yes. But Heaven is not a dream and hotels are not Heaven. Only more work. She will cook for many instead of two. She will earn more money and find more things to need. But," he hesitated, "you do not read well."

"I would study harder if I could stay here."

"If you wanted to study harder nothing is stopping you. Read in the evening. Practice every day."

The boy was warmed by old Simon's mild scolding. "I will practice."

"Sit down now and eat."

They sat at the shaded end of a metal equipment shed. On blustery days the steel sides and giant doors crooned at the breezes. Today the steel was barely ticking in the sunshine as the boy placed his sack in the sand, withdrew the lunch and set it out on the upturned bucket prepared for their table.

"Is it time?" the boy asked later.

"Three or four days at most. I go to the island this afternoon and speak with the company by telephone." He used his fingers as a fork and scooped squid and sticky rice between his lips. "The harvest will begin."

They ate in silence awhile, sharing goat's milk from a scuffed plastic bottle. Finally the boy said, "I'll walk back with you. First I swim to find conch for Grana. Do you think there are sharks now on the grass flats?"

"Later in the afternoon," he answered, drinking. "Watch for shadows on the sand."

"I'm not afraid."

"No. You're not afraid." The old man smiled and handed him the bottle. "Once when I was much younger, when I had been here only a few years, a shark was trapped inside Dam Two. I found him in the morning after heavy weather and he was a large animal, much of his back high out of the water.

"I watched him struggle in the shallow water of the evaporation dam and after while took pity on him. He was dying. I thought too of the prize. The skin, oil, meat, the teeth I would polish and sell. In my mind I planned how his heavy body could be moved from the dam and where I would butcher him. Then I did a foolish thing.

"I entered the water, climbing inside the dam with a hook and chain. I meant to drag him out alive so the meat wouldn't spoil. His struggles were growing weaker and I felt strong. Swimming was difficult for such a large animal in the shallow water, no more than knee deep. I was sure he couldn't arouse himself and come against me.

"The chain and hook were heavy. The chain was coiled on my shoulder thus, and the hook I carried in my hand. The water was cool from the night and freshened by the storm."

The old man paused in his narrative and addressed the boy. "Do you know the tiger shark?"

"The name."

"Not a large shark, perhaps the length of a small dingy, and the head is tiny compared to the body. The back humps to the dorsal fin, and the fin is small too, and appears fine, flimsy, more like a rag in the water. The teeth protrude from the mouth in the tiny head and the white eyes with black dots at their centers are set close to the nose.

"With money from this animal I'd buy rum and beer, a place to keep it cool, and rubber shoes from the island when I went there to eat and be with a woman." He grinned at the boy. "I was young. My toes gripped the sand and the trapped shark tossed in the shallows as I came to kill him.

"I saw his hard eye clearly. The barnacles and scars on his back. A remora longer than a man's arm hung limp at the side of his belly.

"My steps were slow in the water and I saw the animal move his tail. I stopped because the movement was not a struggle. It had purpose. I began to back up. Again the tail. My steps lengthened. In water no deeper than the height of this bucket, the shark accelerated with the swiftness of a fast skiff and the water boiled around him."

The old man chuckled and shook his head, eyes alight. "I was afraid and stumbled from the chain, fell and kicked back against the water. I left the chain but the hook remained in my hand as I ran back, like a crab. Only the fear, maybe God, made it possible for me to reach the dam before the animal, and I crawled onto the earthen top. The shark's tail, a thing of limitless power, lifted him from the water. His lips rolled to expose his teeth. Eyes like glass eyes looked into mine. Beyond his teeth a dark place few men see and survive, and I sat frozen. We were no further apart than you and I. Then his mouth filled with sand and dirt. The tail stopped and he died on the sand looking into me.

"For years I wore his tooth around my neck. Now, I put such things away." He sucked dark sauce from his fingers. "The importance of life diminishes with age. Twice more sharks came inside. Once in the storm canal, too. These I shot with the rifle that is in the shed. More than once I shot them and even then I waited hours before I approached."

The boy stepped inside the shed and returned with fins and an oval face mask. "I'm not afraid," he declared.

Simon smiled. "You are a good boy, Medo. Do you think I told you the story to make you afraid?"

"No," he said. "But I am not."

"Always thus. Remember, trouble comes when things are easy, but I'm glad you're not afraid. Go now, get the conch. We leave soon. I must get the boat to the island and return in time to eat this supper the large woman prepares."

"She wants you should bring money."

"For the rent?"

"Yes."

"If I have enough after the boat she will be paid."

The boy trotted along the dam toward the sea. He was not afraid but pictured the tiger shark in his mind's eye and wondered how a beast with a tiny head could eat a man. Did it take many bites and chew like a dog or swallow them whole like a snake? It was a curious thing.

The island and neighboring cay were miles from any land mass, the surrounding sea always close at hand. During heavy weather the cay was uninhabitable, but always it returned when the water receded, the dams and pans repaired. Rugged reefs and shifting sand flats kept the sea at bay. It was a resilient place and salt had been collected and harvested on the cay for almost three hundred years.

Pirates came to the island in wooden warships, then planters, slaves, adventurers, drug dealers, sailboaters, hippies and tourists. Island people lived on in humble wooden houses built haphazardly on the lee side away from the wind and heavy storm seas, but there was no town. Here and there someone opened a store, a cafe, fish stall. Another would sew or repair what had broken or tell a fortune. There was strong drink and women to love you, but most of the young people left for larger places when they were grown and seldom returned except to bring their parents and grandparents away with them. Only the failures came back to stay.

The cay was even more deserted. A scattering of inhabitants, mostly fishermen and their families. The young men left the cay and the island before they were twenty. Medo knew he would be alone here, or nearly so, if he determined to stay. Old Simon could not live forever, Grana said.

His gaze rested on the horizon as he walked, a straight line of blue on blue. At the furthest boundary of his vision, a white speck. A sail or a ship well out to sea.

Medo kicked his sandals into the air and tossed his shirt and shorts after them before entering the water. He spit into the mask and rubbed the saliva carefully, even into the edges where the glass faceplate joined the silicone. Then he rinsed the mask and sat in the shallows pulling on his fins. The snorkel would have to be wedged between his head and the mask strap. He'd broken the keeper and had no where to buy another.

The water was lukewarm and he scanned the flats for shadows. There were none.

Mossy backs camouflaged the conch in the mixed white sand, turtlegrass, and small hard coral beds, where the transparent pink anemones clung like miniature elephant trunks waving in the surge.

Two conch would be enough. Grana diced them warm with sea water - he kept them alive in a brine water bucket - and they ate them raw with spicy red pepper sauce. Besides rice and beans, they ate from the sea. On Sunday there was chicken.

Twice he dove down and came back with hermit crabs in conch shells, then stole a live one from a small octopus but when he turned it to see the animal inside, the octopus snatched it back. He laughed, swallowed water and was forced to the surface.

Then he spotted two even larger shells almost side by side. He got them both in one dive and swam to shore on his back, the two conch loose and rattling on his bare brown belly.

The sun had already dropped from its zenith and he turned for a last glance at the sea before finding the old man, who would be impatient now to catch his boat to the island. The white speck that had been on the horizon was a yacht or large sport fishing boat. Its course had straightened, set directly for the cay.

Medo slipped into his shorts and tied the conch inside his shirt until he could find a bucket. The white boat was moving at high speed, its bow lifted, curling white in the sunshine. He knew there were sandbars and submerged reefs even some distance from shore and large boats rarely came closer than a mile or more to the cay. He worried that the captain of this vessel didn't know the waters.

The shallow bay where he hunted was protected by a barrier reef several blocks long, not closing the sea from the sand but gating it like a spillway so the aquamarine of the shallows and the deep blue sea seemed separate bodies joined almost by chance. The reef was rock, hard corals. Elkhorn rose in gigantic geometric forests inches below the surface and fiberglass couldn't survive it.

The white boat came on at the same speed. Medo saw a flag - red, white, and blue - high on a mast above the flying bridge. He shaded his eyes and saw the figure of a woman. She appeared tall and erect, her yellow hair flying behind her like the flag.

He wanted to speak. Warn her off.

He dropped the conch and waved, using both arms to indicate danger. The boat was bearing down on the barrier reef, its throttle wide open, bow high. He saw blue along the keel and white water sprayed out yards from both sides.

Medo couldn't make out the woman's face clearly but she seemed expressionless, staring not at the cay or the reef with which she was about to collide, but far off at some distant place. Maybe the island beyond or the continuing sea on the other side. He was helpless and began to shout but the sound died in his throat and he watched in silence as the white boat struck the reef, lifted, twisted, came well across into the bay, slowed and began to sink.

Medo's first instinct was to swim out to the woman but fear held him still as he watched the misshapen boat settle into the bay and fuel spread across the water. The woman was no longer on the flying bridge and he didn't see her in the water. It was quiet. He stood very very still and waited, then turned and ran for the old man.

Darlene Sheets did not expect to die. It came as a surprise, much as the reef and the little cay was a surprise. The impact flung her body hard against the helm and she banged a knee, crying out as the yacht was gutted first by the elkhorn and then the rock corals. This flinging did not kill her.

Darlene was a strong girl and an athlete in her own right before marrying one. Too young, her parents said. Too naive, she said, later. And she made it down from the flying bridge to the salon, where she had gone for a reason she couldn't remember. Maybe to retrieve something? She was stunned and confused and went further below deck to find her belongings in the stateroom she had used during the crossing - not their stateroom because she'd never use that again. The water was rising below and much of what had been in order and in place was contorted, deformed, sharpened.

She slipped and a piece of something pushed through her calf and out again. It lodged in muscle but alongside the bone and a few seconds before the blood and pain, she stared down at it and saw how it had pierced her. The boat twisted again, she staggered and fell. Like a cotter pin, the thing in her leg folded and she was fastened while the water began to rise.

She groped for something sharp with which to cut her calf muscle but there was nothing. She ripped the skin from her hands tearing at the metal, prayed and cursed and lifted her chin when the water reached her mouth finally. Even under the water she watched her own spittle float in oblong gobs from her mouth as she coughed and gagged seawater.

Medo found Old Simon in one of the sheds gathering his things for the crossing to the island. He hadn't seen the white boat and they hurried back to the beach, the boy often running ahead.

"There was a woman," Medo repeated.

"You saw no man, only a woman?"

"Yes."

"A strange thing." The old man shaded his eyes. "These rich white men use women as decorations on the boats. They wish to be admired as captains and I have never seen them without the women or the helm in their hands. A woman alone is a strange thing. We go into the water."

"Now? Without a boat?"

"It isn't too deep and I can still swim for some time without tiring." He smiled in a sad way. "She may be injured. It's important to hurry. Later, if we need the small boat, I'll send you. Bring your mask and the fins. Can you do this?"

"Yes."

They waded into the water to their waists and swam steadily until they reached the stern of the boat, which was partially submerged. It was obvious that the boat rested on the sand now and could sink no further. The flying bridge was clear of the water, the maindeck awash, the sliding glass doors of the salon missing. Inside, they could make out white carpeting that swayed like sea grass inches below the surface.

The old man rested at the stern a moment, then climbed aboard. "Wait," he told the boy when they reached the deck. "Be still a moment."

"Do you hear something?"

"Be very cautious now. Look. Listen. Touch nothing."

"Do you want me to wait here?"

"No. Stay beside me. We must find the woman." He ran his hand along the boy's shoulder. "We might find more. Women often have children with them."

"These kind of women?"

"Maybe not. Come now."

The yacht rested upright, listing to starboard enough to slant the deck. Medo's bare toes gripped the teakwood decking and they waded ahead toward the salon in water just greater than ankle deep.

The old man gripped his arm. "Climb up to the space above and see if the woman is still there," he ordered. "Don't touch her."

Medo climbed. There was no woman. No blood. The throttles were set forward.

"She's gone," he called down.

"She may be in the water."

"I didn't see her go in the water. The boat came across and she was gone."

"We look inside," the old man said.

Medo swung down.

The salon was splendid. One large room with a flat television screen, stereo equipment, leather couches and chairs, rich tables, lamps, inlaid bookcases spilling bound books and CDs. The walls were lavishly paneled in dark wood and hung with colorful paintings of seascapes. A gleaming green fern hung from a ceiling planter and the water lapped discreetly against a marble-topped bar. Medo never imagined such opulence in a boat. "Is this how they live?" he questioned the old man.

"Who?"

"The Americans."

Simon shrugged. Realized then the boy was awed by it.

"Remember why we are here," he said.

A colorful world globe floated against the starboard paneling.

"The woman is gone," Medo said.

"Yes."

"Can we get someone from the island?"

"We will look more," Simon said.

"Where?"

Simon pointed to the submerged steps leading down forward to the berthing areas.

"She was on the top," Medo said. "Why would she come here?"

"We look."

Simon moved to the steps but Medo held his place. When the old man turned to coax him, the boy said, "I think that's her." He pointed above, to the wall.

The forward bulkhead of the salon was covered in photographs, most askew, a few missing, one broken on the flooded deck. "This?" Simon questioned, indicating the fine head of a woman with yellow hair.

"Yes."

"You saw her face?"

"The hair."

They examined the photographs. Sporting and fishing. Many were images of this same woman with a man, then two men smiling above a large cup held before them, another with an elderly couple. One with a dog of an angular breed Medo had never seen. He reached into the water and lifted the broken picture from the deck, a younger close-up of her and the man. He thought it might be a wedding picture but she wore no veil and he only a dark suit. The glass had been smashed and the frame broken in several places as if it had been struck against something again and again.

"What do they call that game?" the old man asked, still staring at the photo wall.

"Volleyball."

"I never remember it," he said. "Do they play it for money?" He was gazing at a trio of photos in which the blonde woman was playing the game and the years were printed at the bottom of each.

"Money?"

"Do they get paid? Do they bet like with horses?"

"I don't know."

"She appears strong." He turned to the boy. "Put the mask on. I go first down the steps until the water is too deep. You swim from there and look for her. Don't go too far from me. If she's not there we will go to the island."

Medo said, "I'm not afraid."

Water had flooded most of the lower deck. The bow section of the boat had born the brunt of the collision. The fiberglass and supporting plywood was ripped in a way that made it look peeled. A large section of the bow hull was missing and that caused the yacht to be down by its bow and burrowed into the sand. As they moved farther from the steps and along the passageway leading to the staterooms the water grew deeper until Simon was up to his chest.

"I can't go ahead," he said. "Look first in this hallway, then the rooms. You will have to hold your breath to go inside the rooms. One at a time only. I know you are a strong swimmer and hold your breath well, but this is different. This is not open water. Things can catch you. One room, then back to me. Understand?"

"Yes."

"This is important, Medo. Do you understand me?"

"Yes, Señor. One room and back to you."

"Exactly."

Before he moved away from Simon, Medo floated in the hallway until his eyes adjusted to the dim light and he could see the deck clearly. The deck had buckled and it was strewn with debris. No dead lady.

He inhaled and exhaled several times before holding a breath and diving down. He swam forward to the farthest stateroom first. The door was gone and the door frame was bowed. Inside, a large bed, dresser, two cushioned chairs, a tall wardrobe of dark wood, and carpeting littered with lamps and bookends, a set of keys and sunglasses. Articles of clothing suspended in the water, swaying like jellyfish in a current. The woman was not here.

Medo surfaced for air.

The old man stood near the stairs, out of the water to his waist. His forehead was furrowed and his mouth set.

Medo inhaled and swam into the second stateroom along the hallway. Inside the light was better, a pale yellow from the sun reflected in the sand through a gaping hole and gathered in the golden hair of the woman who floated like a carnival balloon attached by one leg to a long, jagged strip of metal. Her eyes were open and she was surprised. Medo was not frightened. He felt only sadness and regret as if she might've been someone whom he'd loved.

He settled to the bottom and rested a moment, his knees brushing the swaying carpet. He watched the woman. She shifted slowly in the surge and her hair was alive with light and color, dancing above her in golden waves. He saw how she'd dressed simply in a white, sleeveless T-shirt and plain shorts. Her feet were bare and the toes painted red. The right leg was deformed by the metal that held her and he could see the white bone and dark meat of her muscle. She was so clearly dead Medo felt her peace, and he thought then he could hold his breath all day.

When he returned to the old man he had an emptiness, a bubble inside that he couldn't speak about.

"She is there," he said plainly.

"Dead."

"Yes. Dead."

"We will go to the island."

The trip was uneventful and after they spoke with Constable Ebanks, his second cousin, Medo felt cheated, as if he'd given up something priceless for a pittance. He didn't want to share the woman or the circumstance of her death with anyone except old Simon and the sea around the cay. He remembered too, that she had salt crystals glittering in her eyelashes.

The days that followed were stifling hot, filled with peculiar events that seemed to him like acting. As if the event of this woman's death must somehow be played at and explained after the fact so as to ignore the fact.

It was finally determined she had committed a suicide. Driven the boat into the reef to cause her own death. An unfaithful husband, they said, had driven her to grief and anger. She'd destroyed herself and the boat on which they were spending a vacation. And within days the boat was towed away to scrap, the body of the woman flown to the United States, and the cay left to the salt pans. People talked, and talked, and turned to other topics.

Medo was dissatisfied. He'd been part of something that shook him deep inside and when he saw how people outside - those who hadn't seen the woman die - how they explained it away and found reasons for it and made such great sense of it, then he felt cheated all over again.

The day before harvest he squatted beside the old man on the lip of Dam Four. "Do you believe what they say?" he asked Simon. "That she was suicide?"

"No," he shook his head.

"Why do they say it?"

"It's convenient. Makes them able to go on without her. Easy to blame someone who takes her own life, if you need this."

"Need it?"

"The dead need nothing."

"What happened then, do you think?" The boy looked closely into the old man's face.

"I don't know. Maybe the husband was unfaithful and she was angry, or sad, and took the boat to run away." He gazed out across the evaporating water to the sea beyond. "Maybe she didn't know how to drive a boat or the cay and the island merged in her vision and she misjudged the distance. Any number of things, I suppose. But who commits a suicide by running a boat into a reef? Ha! Foolishness. It was only bad luck killed her, not the cay. We should have carried her weeping onto the beach. This Constable Ebanks is a fool, your cousin."

"I know, but he is older."

"And fond of himself."

"But the American?"

"The unfaithful husband? He maybe thinks it's a fitting end. Rich men have insurance. He has other women. I doubt he will grieve long. Your cousin may even get a nice tip if he writes the death was an accident. Life will go on."

The boy thought about what the old man said. "Life will go on," he repeated. "Not for her."

Simon placed a hand on the boy's shoulder. "Remember? I asked you if you were ready for this. To see this. Death is more than just a body. It's an event." He smiled. "But anyway, this is nothing to us. These aren't our people and they come here and go away again." His hand dropped back onto the dike and he closed it around the salty sand, sifting it through his fingers.

"I was the only one there," the boy said. "When she died. Just me and her."

"Ah."

"Don't laugh at me. I miss her."

"You're a fine boy, Medo. I don't laugh. You lost your mother at a young age and now you witness this thing and it settles into your heart. Maybe it hurts you more than those who said they loved her.

Who can say?"

"I wonder if she saw me there on the beach with the conch. Maybe she said to herself there's a boy there."

"She was looking farther on, I think. She didn't see you."

"It's hard to know what to believe."

"I believe in God," Simon said. "And salt."

"Salt?"

"Salt provides the buoyancy upon which life floats, a basic thing like water or air. Kingdoms were once traded for it and its value was greater than gold. Now it's common, and cheap. People have forgotten." The old man smiled at the boy. "In another time we might have been kings."

"I am the salt king," the boy proclaimed.

"Don't tell your grandmother. Let's go eat."

Harvest was the most exciting time. The layers of salt deep on the pan floor. Machines moved it to the conveyor belt, onto trucks that carried it away to be washed and piled before refining. Medo was sad about the woman, impatient for the harvest, afraid about the hotel, and proud of his part in all of it. Salt was common and cheap - he knew that - but essential too. Without salt life is stale, and Medoro Ebanks was surrounded by salt.

© Originally published in "The Caribbean Writer" Vol. 21, 2007

Green Banana Man

The fat pregnant white woman braced her legs, one against the door and the other against the dash, protecting her bouncing belly as the small gray sedan negotiated a goat trail road through broken countryside. There was a little red-headed girl in the backseat holding tightly onto the hand of a dark young maid with an afro. The man driving the car, Clive Mosby, gripped the wheel two-handed in the manner of an exhausted man clinging to a rope strung across a deep gorge.

Patricia, pregnant and churlish, wore pink shorts with an elastic panel to accommodate her heaving stomach, and above, a pink, sweat-soaked blouse slapped at her chest in the breeze. The outfit was crisscrossed with a dizzy brown plaid. "I cannot take any more of this," she told the man.

"What do you want me to do?" Mosby said. "Turn around? It's just as far back as it is to go on. What's the point?"

"The point is I'm going to deliver this damn kid."

"I've never seen roads like this. I didn't even know there were roads like this. What's the matter with the government in this country?"

"Clive! Just stop the bouncing."

"How? I can stop the car. We can rest awhile."

"No!" she said. "This was stupid. Go on. *Just go on!*"

The tiny trunk held provisions for their day at the beach. Melon on ice and red wine, warming in a cheap cooler alongside a plastic bucket and sand shovel for the little girl; and blankets, towels, suntan lotions. There was beer, leftover chicken, potato salad, oranges, dill pickles and small sandwiches made with guava jam. Four mangos.

The narrow road was fenced on both sides. The fence was living cactus. Beyond, were herds of goats and Clive knew it didn't just look like a goat trail. He avoided grinning at this. Patricia flew into a rage at his humor; her suffering, rooted as it was, in his uncontrolled urges. She was pregnant barely four years since her other pregnancy and claimed that was having them one right after the other.

"Once we're through these hills," he promised her, "the road levels. Runs along the beach, according to the map, and that should smooth it out."

"This is stupid," she said. "Just stupid."

"It was your idea, you know."

"Oh, I was waiting for that!"

"Well, it's true."

"I don't care. I couldn't sit around that apartment another minute. You have no idea what it's like to be pregnant."

"I know," he admitted.

She pointed ahead. "What's that?"

"A crossroads."

"Oh no. No, no, no."

"Not on the map," he said, stopping the car. "Left or right?"

Patricia clamped her right hand to the back of her neck, rotated her head clockwise, sighed, and crossed her forearms under her weighted breasts.

In the backseat no one spoke. The little girl, Marie, grew quiet whenever her parents spoke sharply. The maid, Rosa, struggled to keep from smiling. How did they get lost on an island? Just drive until you see someone and ask. How did they think people found their way around? And maybe there is an interesting man with a motorbike. ¡Qué ingenuidad!

"I'm going right," Mosby decided. "Go down here a few miles. See if we can't get out of these hills or up high enough on one to see the ocean. Got to be here somewhere. If that doesn't work, we'll go back and try the other fork. Since there are only two possibilities, one has to be right. Right?"

Patricia refused to answer. She was trying not to cry, or not let him see her. Riding made her nauseous, even though that was supposed to have faded by now, and she had to go to the bathroom because she almost always had to go to the bathroom. It was hot and sticky so you drank quarts of water and then you had to go to the bathroom because of the pressure. She'd explain it to him, he'd understand and stop and then say afterward something like, "Well, you ought to be good for another first down. Ten more yards."

He had not driven the car forward. "Did you hear what I said?" he asked.

"Yes."

"Well?"

"By all means, turn right."

"Well, it's either left or right."

"I know."

"So I have to go one way or the other. I can't go both ways at the same time."

"I know."

"If we do go right, and it's the wrong way, then we have to come back."

"Yes."

"Then you're going to be mad because I took the wrong way."

"I'm going to be mad *either* way."

"So how can I win?"

"You can't. Shut up and drive."

He shifted, eased ahead and shifted again to second. Dust filtered in through the cracks and openings, vents and windows. She thought it tasted faintly burnt or volcanic. If this was a road to anywhere, why hadn't they seen other traffic?

Mosby knew he couldn't win. Lost the minute he agreed to take her to Las Salinas Beach. They'd never been outside the city, hadn't had the car a week. Already in trouble. Didn't speak the language. Alone here. He hadn't driven a stick since he was a kid making restaurant deliveries in Dad's pickup. They weren't even driving an American car - a British Morris Minor 1000. Who named a car "Minor" anything? Cars had names like Mustang, Ram Charger, Barracuda; not Minor. Didn't they have a Mini, too? No wonder the Brits lost their empire. They were effeminate automakers.

The road, a battlefield of barrage craters, rocked the car no matter how carefully he eased it into them and up the other side. The little transmission ground and the tires snapped at the stones and everyone was jostled. The four-cylinder engine struggled. He was thankful for the dust. If the craters had been filled with water, or if it rained now, they'd be drowned.

At the top of the next hill he stopped.

"Now what?" she asked.

"I'm going to climb the fence and walk up there," he pointed. "Might see the ocean from there."

"Okay. I'm going to pee."

Someone told him the island didn't have poisonous snakes but it had plenty of large brown lizards and green lizards and transparent lizards. They rustled in the tall brown grass and sometimes sat up on stones and flicked their tongues. They were accompanied by some kind of invisible insects that mewled in unison like a steel guitar, but louder, without the pitch slide. The ground seemed to crawl and scream at him as he walked on it.

At the crest of the hill he stopped. In all directions were more hills, strange trees he thought should be growing in Africa not here, and big white birds with vulture necks. No ocean.

He turned back to the car. Patricia was squatting by the rear tire, on the wrong side. "Nothing but more hills," he called down. She ignored him and he turned back to the hills. The road wound through them in what seemed a downward track. Maybe it did lead to the sea.

When they went on, it was a long time before anyone spoke. The sun was high in the sky now and oppressive heat covered them like dust and brought sweat out from every pore in a manner Patricia had never thought possible. She didn't sweat. Her face flushed, her head ached, her body seemed alive with pins and needles, but she didn't sweat. Now she was sweating from every part of her. Sticking to the vinyl seat, the underside of her forearms, her palms, behind her ears, the trembling place her breasts rested on her belly. She didn't trust herself to speak.

Clive Mosby had been right about the downward track of the goat trail road. It meandered through the creases in the hills like an eroded stream bed and finished up in a swamp. It seemed to Clive that they had made a transition from desert to jungle in little more than a heartbeat, crossing some invisible bridge from Saharaland to Amazonland.

He couldn't see ten feet into the brush that suddenly crowded both sides of the track. Instead of straightening out now that there were no hills, the road began to snake through the undergrowth, tall weeds and canopied trees, as if its builders had been lost. Drunk, more likely, but there were no bumps. The road was packed sand, gray and wet. Patricia was not complaining. The smell of rotting vegetation, the sound of gurgling, the realization that all the tangled branches overhanging them might not be branches but writhing nonpoisonous snakes hanging by their tails, and the lack of sunlight gave them the shivers. Windows cranked shut on both sides of the car.

Rosa, the maid, spoke for the first time since they became lost. "This is not correct," she told them in Spanish.

Clive had no idea what she was saying since he didn't speak the language. "What'd she say?" he asked Patricia.

"'No correcto.' Figure it out," his wife said.

How was he supposed to figure that out? Anyway, he wasn't backing up. The road led to something, even if it was a crocodile farm.

He sniffed something metallic coming from beneath him, behind the firewall. Burning rubber or hot rust. He knew it was related to the little car. The overloaded, fifteen-year-old, all-they-could-afford little car. He pressed on the accelerator and shifted to third. Whatever happened now, it wasn't going to happen here in the swamp. Somewhere ahead must be sunshine.

They flew out suddenly onto acres of sand dunes and sea grass. Clive smiled and the little girl said, "Oh! Lookit!"

"The ocean," Patricia said. But there was no ocean, just sand and grass and heat from the sun.

The windows came down.

The trail led further to the right, angling and twisting into the dunes. A good trail, hard-packed and distinct. Clive thought he smelled ocean and he told them.

"I can't smell anything," Patricia said. "I haven't been able to smell anything for nine months. When I do smell something, I puke."

"Daddy," the little girl said. "Why is there smoke coming out the front of the car?"

He should've noticed that but he hadn't noticed it. He'd been looking far ahead, expecting any second to round a dune and pop out onto a beach. The car was smoking and the smell was even stronger than before. "Damn it!" he said.

"Damn it!" the little girl said.

"Watch your mouth, Clive," Patricia cautioned.

He stopped the car and got out. Under the hood smoke blew from around the radiator cap, hissing and spitting. He fanned it away. Half way down the radiator's bug-coated surface, a dime-sized hole gushed steam and orange water.

He walked back to the driver's side window and leaned in to address the occupants. "Radiator's got a hole in it."

"Meaning what?" Patricia asked.

"Meaning we're in big trouble."

"Okay," she said. "Find a garage."

"Are you kidding? We can't even find the Atlantic Ocean."

The maid patted the little girl's cheek and climbed from the backseat. "Espera un minuto," she told them. "Espera." She stepped around the front of the car and stretched out both arms, palms out. "Esperame." Then she turned and jogged away up the trail.

"What's that all about?" Clive asked.

"She's probably just had it," Patricia said. "I'd run myself if I wasn't so fat."

"Well, she isn't going to find anything. Whole place reminds me of Africa. Jungle and desert. Where's the white sand and turquoise water? So far the only palm trees I've seen were in the city in somebody's yard."

"You've never been to Africa. Can't you drive the car a little bit?"

"A little bit? How do you drive a car a little bit?"

"You know, slow. Take it easy. Be gentle."

Clive sighed. "I was only in third gear. About twenty miles per hour. Can't be more than a few cups of water left in that radiator now."

"Well," she said. "We can't just sit here."

"Fine. I'll move it ahead in low. Once we go a few feet and it starts boiling again, we'll have to stop. If we don't, we'll blow the engine. Then we'll all be totally esperame, or whatever it is."

They jerked along in low and managed to cover quite a distance among the dunes before the engine overheated again, spitting and smoking. They stopped. Waited. Went on.

Just shy an hour of this, as they sat waiting for their next lunge forward, a crowd of multi-colored people charged them from the top of a dune. They were shouting, pointing, urging each other on toward the car.

"Wow," the little girl said. "People."

Leading the charge, Clive recognized their maid Rosa. Patricia had hired her only two weeks ago because they couldn't live in the country without permanent supervision. Their apartment had no washer, dryer, dishwasher, garbage disposal or dependable electricity. No phone, no screens on the windows to keep the bugs out but plenty of lizards to eat them and the lizards lived behind the pictures on the walls. Rosa bought their food, cooked it, and in all manner of daily living, cared for them. Patricia said that if she lived through her delivery there was every chance the baby would have to be given to the maid for it to survive. So Clive felt that now it was a good omen that Rosa was leading a shouting foreign army that surrounded his disabled vehicle. One man in particular, repeated a phrase. "Poner en punto muerto."

"Do you understand that?" Clive asked Patricia.

She shrugged.

The crowd, which included men, women and children of all ages, surrounded the little car and some pushed it from behind. It was in gear and didn't move, only rocked. "Tell them to quit that," Patricia said.

"They're trying to push us."

The maid reached inside, across Clive's lap, and jiggled the shifter. "Punto muerto," she said.

"Put it in the dead spot. Neutral," Patricia ordered.

The crowd took turns pushing and within half an hour they arrived in a dirty little village on the sand. Acres of sand. Few trees or dunes. Flat, brown-gray sand and maybe two dozen homemade houses the size of tool sheds, all built from cast-off materials - plastic, cardboard, plywood, branches, tin and driftwood. They sat in barbed wire, fenced yards. Each seemed to shelter a dozen or more people from infancy to dotage. Every yard had a goat and chickens.

Children ran alongside the disabled car, peeking in at the white occupants and laughing. The pushers halted at a house with a tree in its yard. The tree was not in leaf, but several chairs and an unpainted wooden table were set out under its naked branches. Between the tree and the yard gate, a large woman stood ready to receive them.

Clive and Patricia climbed from the car without a word. The little girl took her mother's hand and they went into the yard.

No one followed and Clive noticed they'd all fallen silent.

Inside, the woman gave a speech. Everyone listened respectfully. Clive recognized the word *bienvenido* because he'd seen it on a banner at the airport and knew it meant welcome. He was pleased to be welcomed somewhere, even if he had no idea where. He still hadn't seen an ocean.

The speechmaking concluded. Several people clapped and all were smiling. The door to the house flew open and two younger women appeared carrying highly varnished wooden trays. Two coffees on the first tray, alongside a charred two-pound coffee can that served as the pot. Both unmatched cups were without handles, their rims badly chipped. There was sugar and condensed milk in two wooden bowls. The second tray was placed before the little girl. A warm bottle of Coca Cola.

Most of the crowd fell silent again as the coffee and soda was served. Clive believed they were all waiting to see what might happen next. Would the foreigners drink the coffee? And if they did, would they like it? He felt a bit like a specimen but appreciated the weight of the moment.

He lifted the cracked crockery to his lips, with what panache he could muster, and drank solemnly. Withdrawing the cup, he raised an eyebrow, smiled, and said in a deep voice, "Excellent!"

A moment later the word "excelente" was repeated several times and Clive Mosby had an unnamed village in the palm of his hand. They sat under the tree for the better part of an hour and were served numerous delicacies, most of which were so sweet they hurt his teeth.

Patricia wore her first smile of the day. Marie had gone off with the children. Rosa regaled the single girls with stories of living in close proximity to white foreigners. Or at least that's what Clive thought she was doing. He could've gone on like that for some time but noticed a group of men trying to get the hood up on his car.

"Hold it there!" he said, trotting over.

A group of eight or nine surrounded him, talking and gesturing. One short man still worked at the hood. "Quit that," Clive ordered. "It's the radiator."

"¿Que?" a man asked.

"Radiator," Clive said. He stepped around to the driver's side, popped the hood latch and repeated, "Radiator," then lifted the hood and pointed to the hole.

"Ahh," they said, nodding.

The short man reached inside, inserted his little finger in the hole, pulled it back out and examined it. Several others examined the man's little finger, too. Clive joined them.

Heated discussion ensued. Clive was included but never knew whether to nod or disapprove anything. He was afraid they might begin ripping at the engine and he was relieved to see they had no tools. He guessed they were discussing the best way to fix the radiator, but could've been discussing who to send for a mechanic, if there was such a thing nearby.

Patricia was attracted by the deliberations and arrived barefooted. "Where are your sandals?" Clive asked her.

"I haven't felt this good in months," she said. She made a crooked smile and kissed his cheek.

"We're stranded among strangers in an unknown place. We can't find the ocean. Our car is busted and it can't be fixed. We don't speak the language, have a limited amount of money and in a few hours it will be dark."

"They put rum in my coffee," she said, and strolled back toward the yard scuffing the sand with her painted toes.

One of the men grabbed at Clive's shirt sleeve. "Plátano verde!" he exclaimed, and pointed at the radiator. Those around him nodded. Clive knew the word plátano because it was the second word he'd learned in Spanish. The first was huevos - eggs. He learned it his first morning on the island at almost exactly five o'clock. A man in the street, balancing at least ten flats of eggs on his head was shouting the word and whenever a maid came out from one of the houses to buy some, he'd hop-step and all those flats of eggs would jump perfectly from his head into his outstretched arms and it was the damnedest thing Clive Mosby had ever seen in his life. He thought huevos was a great word. Plátanos however, was a bad memory because he made the mistake of calling a plátano a green banana. He did this in a restaurant to the amusement of everyone at his table. They had all been there long enough to know a plantain from a banana.

Clive wasn't necessarily a prideful man, but the public humiliation stung him in a new environment where he was already unsure of himself and trying desperately to be accepted. He refused to eat plantain thereafter, even in soup, and often called it a green banana just for spite. After all, it looked like one. Unless you looked closely.

The islanders ate plantain like North Americans eat potatoes. They boiled it or fried it green in peanut oil and called it tostones. They let it ripen, turn yellow and black, and ate it sweet. It was in soup, stew, rice, sauces, and a side dish at every restaurant. A local company even marketed plantain chips in plastic bags. It was everywhere, a staple of life. While his newly-acquired friends joked about it, Clive felt the green banana was a personal burden, and ate potatoes or rice.

The crowd around the nose of Clive's car had fallen silent. A woman had arrived with a long knife and a green plantain. She slit the plantain several times lengthwise and peeled it. The peelings were tossed in the sand.

The short man spread his arms and called for the crowd to step back and give them room. He positioned himself by the grill and another man lined up behind him. The woman ran a dirty thumbnail along the length of the pale yellow plantain, now that it had been peeled exactly like a green banana, and its meat rolled in a thin spool against her thumb. She flipped this gob into the waiting, cupped hands of the short mechanic's helper, and repeated it until the gob was the size of a tennis ball. The mechanic layered it carefully into the hole in Clive's radiator, like packing the sore cavity of an excised tooth.

When he realized what they were doing, Clive left.

He went back into the yard and found Patricia. She was sitting with her legs spread, wiggling her bare toes and drinking rum-laced coffee.

"They're slopping green bananas into the radiator," he told her.

"Good," she said.

"Where's Marie?"

"I don't know. Playing, I guess."

"You might want to find her, don't you think? Though we'll most likely never get out of here."

"I don't care," Patricia said, smiling into her cracked cup. "This is the most fun I've had since we got to this country. These are good people. Warm."

"How do you know? You can't even speak to them."

Patricia smiled up at him and she didn't appear drunk, just blissful. "Sit down by me," she said. "We've talked about the

weather and kids. About being pregnant. Pain of delivery. Joy of
new life. We've talked about love and food and men. We act out our
lives and it works almost better than talking. I've got a recipe for
some kind of fish, too. Red snapper, I think. We've made ourselves
understood. Started trusting each other. Marie's never been safer in
her life." She patted the back of his hand. "And by the way, ocean's
right there behind us about two hundred yards, where those white
clouds are."

Finally Clive said, "They're putting green bananas in the
radiator."

"I know, Sweetheart. It'll be okay. That's probably what they do
here."

A short time later the plátano patch had hardened, water was
carried in cans from a rain barrel alongside the house and the
radiator refilled. They'd got directions from one of the men who
insisted on riding the fender to show them the beach, which was not
far. Everyone gathered to say goodbye and Clive reached a hand
into his pocket for some cash but Patricia grabbed his arm. "No,"
she said.

"I have to give them something."

"They won't like it. Won't understand it."

"Everybody understands money," Clive insisted.

Patricia smiled at him but her eyes were dark and flinty. "I said
don't." She squeezed his arm, digging in her nails. "Get your hand
out of your pocket."

"What's the matter with you?"

"Clive. This whole village just turned out to fix your stupid car
and used their food and water to do it. Meanwhile, they gave us the
best they had - food, drink, entertainment, even daycare. When's the
last time that happened to you anywhere? Huh?"

He withdrew his hand from his pocket and began shaking hands
with the men. "Okay," he told Patricia. "Adiós," he said to them.
Everyone laughed.

Children ran alongside the car for awhile, shouting. Two older boys jumped onto the rear bumper and rode a distance before hopping clear. He hadn't noticed until then how none wore shoes. There were no fat children. No round-faced chubby ones like at home.

They arrived at the beach within minutes and were surprised to find a parking lot half filled with large American cars, vans, and four-wheel drives. Their guide stuck out his hand, nodded to Clive almost as if he were embarrassed, then hugged Patricia and kissed her on both cheeks before trotting off down the packed-sand trail toward home.

Patricia was crying.

"What's the matter with you?"

"Shut up."

They carried everything to the beach, which stretched for miles in either direction, forming a large crescent bay that glittered and sloshed in the sunshine. There were purple hills across the water and a gentle surf sighing on the sand, packing it, binding it before the next sweep stirred the grains, washed and separated them, rejoined them to others in a timeless embrace.

Reservado

"I'm tired of repeating," she repeated. "I'm going alone."

"No," her daughter said. "You are not!"

Laura waited out the uncomfortable silence. "Don't be a bitch kitty Megan. You and Ken take the girls to the zoo. I need to be alone awhile, okay?" She settled back in the metal patio chair, pleased by the mid-day sun busy atop the water of the bay, polishing it jade. Little but the buildings had changed here and she felt an anticipation to be off, discovering. In a lighter tone she said, "I'm the mother. You're the daughter."

Megan knew she'd overstepped and didn't want to spoil the day, or the vacation. "Fine," she said. "But this isn't 1972, when you lived here. Things change. We don't want anything to happen to you."

Laura smiled. "I'm not in a nursing home yet you know."

Typical, Megan thought. "Okay if I ask *where* you're going?"

That secret Laura must keep. "Visit my ghosts," she said carelessly. "Be nostalgic." She hated her longings, dragging her into a past she'd spent a lifetime trying to forget.

"Ken will be disappointed," Megan predicted. "What about dinner?"

Laura reached across and grasped her daughter's hand. "Ken will survive. Anyway, it's Santo Domingo. Nobody eats before eight or nine. I'll be in the bar at Mesón de la Cava by eight. See you there."

"You *are* stubborn." She returned the squeeze, smiling at last. "Anything's better than yesterday, driving around listening to 'Oh! This used to be like this and that used to be like that.' What a drag! You only lived here a couple years."

"Eight years," Laura corrected. She let go of Megan's hand and sipped her Coke, gone flat. "Those were my best years, Honey." She smiled shyly. "Young, before your father and family. Can't I indulge myself for a few hours? Pretend I'm not plump, my hair isn't colored, that I once jumped into my convertible without opening the door first? Roll your eyes if you like but some things you really can't understand until you're older. Sorry."

"*Please*, Mom."

Laura hoped she hadn't given anything away. She shouldn't have mentioned Brad, her late husband in that way. Megan was no fool and might toy with the possibility of another man in her mother's past. Grown children are often naive in such things.

Fifteen minutes later her taxi merged into the wicked afternoon traffic. In back, Laura Mason concentrated on reclaiming what she'd once seized so effortlessly and held so cheaply. She despised the rhetorical question, *Where did it all go*? but how *does* youth evaporate so quickly? Entirely possible too, she thought, that Megan was right, she might've been better off at the zoo.

The driver, a sullen little man with a sparse goatee, never heard of the Versailles, claimed it didn't exist. Laura spoke to him sharply in halting Spanish, ordering him up Abraham Lincoln to Avenida Bolívar, then west. Nothing ahead but strip malls and a supermarket, the driver bitched. The norteamericana was confused, and by his tone she knew all women were confused.

Laura had tried to keep her Spanish after retiring from State, but they'd finally gone to live in Chicago and there she got out of the habit, remembering words but failing at accent and flavor. She used to feel Dominican, think in Spanish, now she felt like a tourist.

The Versailles was located in an L-shaped strip mall, Centro Comercial Texaco. The Texaco station was the mall's anchor but the cafe occupied the largest space. In the 70s Jack's dive shop was there, and a boutique, auto parts store, offices. She ordered the cab into the parking lot and found the gas station office derelict, its only window cracked, the boutique used for storage, the auto parts store empty and dark, Jack's dive shop a meat market. The bottom of the L, the Versailles, a wreck. Laura gasped and brought the taxi to a halt, tipping the driver more than she'd intended.

The gas station, still operating but unkempt and filthy, seemed to attract loiterers who leered at her more from curiosity than desire. Layers of dripped oil, exhaust, tire marks darkened the cracked concrete. She moved cautiously around the pumps and set out toward the patio portion of the cafe. No one whistled.

Earthen, brick-red planters still outlined the patio, their flowers long dead. A few stunted royal palms remained, weeds, one sad croton surviving on rainwater and luck. Scattered near the building a few tables not worth stealing, several chairs with torn seats. The cafe's smoked glass windows with dark green hand-painted borders, once unique and mysterious, streaked now and soiled. Underfoot, a brown lizard scampered among the dead leaves and she glanced quickly at her bare feet inside the sandals. That morning she'd painted each toe pink to match the pin stripes of her mid-calf skirt. Above, she wore a conservative khaki shirt with epaulets to square her shoulders. It bloused nicely to hide her thickening waist. Even at her most self-critical, she decided the damage done by the years disappeared when she took a deep breath and held up her chest. Lately, she'd gone to a push-up bra and heavier mascara but the green eyes were still sharp, moist, and alight with curiosity. Men did not overlook her. Primping for ghosts, she thought.

There *was* a ghost, of course. He inhabited the place because she brought him along, though he looked better, not having aged a day. Plucking a handful of dried leaves from the litter, Laura Mason rubbed scaly soil from the glass and peered inside at her past.

Laura turned onto El Conde Street as lightning flashed, deepening shadows along the narrow pavement. At first she thought it was the street lights flickering, coming back, but thunder rumbled above the harbor, echoing across the water. She pulled over and flipped the top up.

Rain came without warning, soaking her to the skin before she could lock the soft roof in place. She ducked inside. Raindrops pelted the canvas and grew to rivers in the street, swelling beneath an oily skin of litter heightening the ripe smell of rot. Laura bit at a torn nail and pressed her toes against the clutch.

Traffic was light. She passed the Cathedral of Santa María and wound north away from the Colonial City toward the suburbs. A traffic policemen in gray uniform and white helmet slouched inside the candlelit doorway of a colmado and watched her pass. She barely noticed, hurrying to arrive at the Versailles before Jack so he'd find her seated there at the table waiting. She accelerated. The tiny green car growled at the ancient stone buildings and swept through the wet streets trailing a pink mist.

The cafe appeared deserted when she dashed across the empty patio, pausing to appraise herself in the opaque windows. Behind them, the spatter of diners seemed a shabby lot. Aimless people, suddenly driven indoors by the rain. The cafe's absentee owner was an Air Force General but his status didn't attract what she thought of as a classy clientele. Anyway, she knew the Air Force had more generals then functional aircraft.

She feared that she'd dressed inappropriately, discarding piles of shirts before settling on a simple tube top under a purple silk shirt bought at least a year before Jack. The long-sleeved shirt was nearly puce, the tube white against her tan and the marks left by her spaghetti straps. She tugged at the door. Behind her the metal chairs and tables, the folded umbrellas, reflected the patio lighting. They must be running a planta.

Inside, she glanced to the right. The small white sign with black letters was on the table - *Reservado*. She breathed deeply. The table was empty. Monolito appeared at her elbow and seated her there.

"¿El Señor?" he inquired.

"Poco después," she answered. Her Spanish was flawless and Monolito never spoke English to her, but spoke *only* English to Jack because Jack claimed he couldn't learn any other language.

Monolito was diminutive and stood very erect in a billiard-green waiter's jacket and she knew that when Jack arrived he would assume an air of greater formality. She didn't understand why he liked Jack, a man so painfully North American. The waiter moved behind her and began to dry her long hair with a small towel until she brushed him away and shook her head not unlike a dog. Dark hair, thick, hanging in crumpled waves that layered over and over and billowed from the sides of her head, retaining enough rainwater to drip and dampen her shoulders. She shivered in the air conditioning.

"I'll wait awhile," she said, and Monolito withdrew.

It was pleasant to be alone and wait. She believed strongly in waiting. In patience. Anticipation a finer thing than its expression usually, like believing the soft lies lovers say. Love itself was painful enough. Jack was her first mature love so she thought now that the hurt might just as well go deep, as it's supposed to, and make her remember always and guard the memory for later.

She inhaled the smells from the kitchen - oregano and onions, hot peanut oil and pineappled ham - which were surprisingly clear and Dominican though the Versailles was built to resemble a cafe the

General frequented in Miami. Jack would order the ham. He would study the menu and discuss far too much of it and order the ham.

Her seat at the window offered a fine view of both the wet patio and the main dining area. Two body lengths to her left hung the cafe's only indoor attraction, a lighted birdcage. It hung inside a bookcase room divider that separated the dining area and bar. The mechanical bird inside the cage sang the same three songs again and again. She never tired of the songs nor the hollow plastic bars of the cage, alight with a mysterious pale yellow liquid that bubbled inside and shimmered, casting a phosphorescent, nervous glow. She compared it to the restlessness of the sea and covered her ears once when Jack explained how it worked.

Jack came by taxi. What happened to his truck? He strolled across the lot toward the cafe entrance, wearing the gray double knit trousers that clutched his thighs and made them appear heavy. He had on the old sandals with the big toe loops and a tattered guayabera the color of guacamole. Bareheaded, he walked like there was no rain. She couldn't find a thing wrong with him.

He sat down and he was wet. She said, "You shaved your mustache."

"Didn't want to look like a hippie once I got back to the States."

"It only made you look Dominican."

"So who wants to look Dominican?"

"Dominicans do."

"How about a drink?" he said, avoiding her eyes.

"Is that all you can say?" She waited for his answer and felt heat rising in her cheeks. Jack studied the fan ticking slowly above her head and she watched the blades spinning in his eyes.

He grinned and said, "We'll raise our glasses, toast the past, and spit in the eye of destiny."

"Go to hell, Jack," she said.

"It's only a drink, Laura."

"No it isn't." Her green eyes flashed. "It's an act....this last goodbye. Some sort of staged ending. I wonder sometimes what goes through your head!" She tossed damp hair from her face and flushed. "Now I'm making a spectacle of myself."

Stern and composed, Jack raised an eyebrow and signaled to Monolito. She gained nothing by making a scene, angered that he'd forced it upon her. He spoke spontaneously to strangers after all, spilled personal details of his life that couldn't possibly interest them, but now refused to talk about their own collapse. She felt their love as a common stream. That they were one. And now this drought. This dry desert where nothing flourished but regret and frustration. She fought an impulse to walk out. Put an end to it. Instead, she watched closely as he lit a cigar and waved again at Monolito.

Outside, the downpour continued, washing gullies in the car park, glistening on croton leaves and compelling them to dance wildly below the window. The General had an odd passion for flowers - cattleya orchids, cereus, and pink pompons in the brick planters. Along the stone and steel walls of the courtyard there were cascades of orange bougainvillea, their petals beaten by the rain, littering the tile. Night storms rarely brought wind.

The fresh smell of rain, the sharp sweetness of the General's flowers, were locked out by the tobacco haze and poor ventilation. In the dim light, Laura just made out the dwarfish Monolito in the bar, his back to them, locked in animated conversation with three other green-jacketed waiters she recognized.

Jack began to "pssst" loudly.

"I hate that noise, Jack."

"I want a drink. Pssst! Pssst!"

Monolito's head turned, in unison with a dozen others. He peered at them through the lighted bird-in-a-cage, grinning, fluttering his fingers at Jack. Jack rolled his eyes. "Brain of a sparrow," he said. "Real dumbwaiter."

Laura laughed, too loudly. "You're a cretin," she said. "I love you."

"Very complimentary," he said, "but I appreciate the change in attitude." He looked up as Monolito approached.

"Lo siento, Señor," the waiter said, faking servility. "I have no see you arrival. Drink somesing?"

"SomeTHING, my little Dominican friend, not someSING," Jack scolded. "You sound like a foreigner."

"Sí," he said, smiling. "But the Inglés is a foreign language en la República, no?"

Jack smiled and they were happy. Monolito repeated an off-color joke, which Laura translated. Laura's friends learned the language and tried to fit in. Jack anticipated a national effort to learn his language, accept his views, his superiority. This flaw in anyone else, was somehow character in Jack. She couldn't explain this. Maybe love was blind after all.

"Very amusing, Monolito," Jack said. "Now, how about some service? Usual drinks and bring the menu."

"Sí, Señor." Monolito winked at Laura. "Hors' d'oeuvres'?"

"Later. Drinks now."

Laura watched the little man spin around and dance his way between the tables, singing along with a familiar merengue melody drifting in from the bar. Like Monolito, Laura knew the song's melancholy words and familiar theme of unrequited love set to a quick Latino beat. She stared out at the rain. "I'll never come back here," she said. "After you're gone, I mean."

"Don't be silly."

"You'd think of me here wouldn't you? Sitting at this table, weeping." She shook her head. "Won't happen."

"Just what I wanted tonight, a fight," he said. "Only suggested coming here so we didn't end up in bed."

"Quite a change of pace then, from the last few days."

"Now it's not appropriate."

"Not appropriate?" She looked aside to see if anyone was

listening. "Since when?"

"I didn't mean it that way. Just meant I didn't want to get close to you tonight. Better this way. No last desperate clinging."

He was deciding for her again, like the first time she met him.

Jack was exactly the kind of man she'd avoided - loud, smiley, self-assured. An awful man wearing double-knits and patent leather at Dawn's party, poolside, drink in each hand, grinning, closing in on her. "Hey, Babe." She guessed he was drunk and tried to find a way around him but he blocked her, pressing the attack. "What's the matter? Daddy don't let you talk to strangers?"

He stood too far inside her comfort zone and she had regrettably short legs, often lied about her height. She stared helplessly at his pasty, sockless feet stuffed in the white patent loafers and felt sorry for him. Salmon red trousers and synthetic shirt with lusty orange flowers, unbuttoned to mid-belly, completed the outfit. His teeth matched his shoes and his hair was winged and puffed.

Before she could stop herself she'd said, "My, aren't you the big stud!" She needn't have worried. He wasn't offended.

"Simmer down," he said. "No way to treat a guy who just bought you a drink." He landed the martini in her hand clumsily, spilling some and sucking his knuckles.

"Who are you?" She couldn't help herself.

"John Doubleday, like the book guys. Call me Jack."

"I'll call you Mr. Doubleday."

"Suit yourself, Ms Mason." He dragged the Ms to give it a buzzing noise. "Laura, I believe?"

Anyone could've given him her name, and a cold *excuse me* taken her safely away, but she didn't like giving ground, so she stayed, eyeing him curiously while the moonlight played in his hair and they talked.

"I've seen you before," he said.

"How very special."

"At the Embassy."

"My office is there."

He grinned. "Hate the damn place."

"Oh? Miss your last issue of *Esquire*? And those awful beggars! Why aren't they home cuddling a teddy bear or watching cartoons? Poverty's such a bummer isn't it?"

"Nothing like that," he said, simply. "I need a work permit to run my boat down here."

She listened to his story. She'd heard a hundred like it. Local officials were dishonest, lazy, even belligerent. They purposely spoke no English, begged boldly for bribes and then did nothing once he'd paid. His own people were no better - kept him waiting, shook their heads, shrugged him off. All the while, his boat sat idle, drinking his cash. "Nothing but a hole in the water I pour money into," he said.

Most of that evening she'd treated him badly, verbally sparring, outwitting him and showing him up. After all, it was a diplomat's game. Later, she surprised herself by joining him for a nightcap at that "little place he knew" (a familiar tourist trap along the Malecón) and sat there like a fool listening to palms rustling in the trades and the city slowly fading off to sleep and the sea kissing the sand beneath the sound of their voices until finally a fresh dawn came and she let him kiss her. He was, of course, putty in her hands.

So it happened that elegant Laura Mason, who glided through the narrow streets of the Capital in her sweet convertible, envy of all, became "You know, Jack's girl."

The rain stopped as suddenly as it had begun. The General's flowers glittered quietly in the soft light fanning from the cafe windows. Laura peered out at the dark sky and already saw stars between the patchy clouds. "I can't do this, Jack," she said, still looking away. "I thought I could, but I can't."

Jack slapped his hand flat on the table. "Damn it, Laura! You knew this was coming. You knew I had to go."

"You want to go." Tears now, finally.

"And you want to stay."

There it was in a nutshell, their little dilemma. Her staying, him going. Simple. Easily solved. One of them would give in because they loved each other and both would stay or both go. She knew this and Jack knew it too, so why hadn't it happened?

Jack had his ticket to Miami and still they sat here, waiting to see who loved who the most, or maybe they didn't love each other at all, maybe they just had a six-year-long affair. "I need your handkerchief," she said, subdued.

"Here," he said. "It's clean."

"If you'd taken the money," she said, wiping her nose, "you wouldn't have had to sell the stupid boat."

"Get off it, Laura. I'm not taking money from you. I told the bank they've got the boat back."

"Sorry to talk *sense*."

Monolito arrived, carrying their drinks on a tray which he presented with a royal flourish, sweeping it overhead at breakneck speed, before landing center table.

"Dumb shit," Jack said, smiling. Monolito wagged a finger, bowed and turned away. "Pretending he's somebody."

"We're all pretending," Laura said, gliding a perfect finger around the rim of her glass, feeling the wetness. "You're pretending pride. I'm pretending to be modern."

"Don't talk pride," Jack said. "Pride's a condition, like baldness or something, and being modern is really just stubbornness. You can help it. Kiss off the State Department and come home with me."

She threw the handkerchief across the table. "Any idea what it costs a woman like me to get where I am today? Any idea at all?"

"Don't get me wrong, Laura," he said. "You're better than a man. Better than ten men. That's the tragedy of it. The real tragedy."

"Now I know why you didn't want to talk about pride," she said, stiffly.

"I don't want to talk about any of this crap. I just want to eat dinner and get the hell out of here."

"Fine," she said. "Here's your menu."

His anger quieted her to the point she wished to be invisible, not out of fear but out of failure for becoming the source of it, because for some reason she couldn't bear that. She glanced up at him. His face was hidden behind the menu, pretending to read, but steaming.

Let him stew. She sat perfectly still and kept her back straight and watched the yellow bubbles while the music played. It wasn't anger crippling her, it was frustration, a souring that grew inside them both. What kind of love did they share if it failed them now?

After a long time she said, "Jack, put the menu down and look at me." She waited until he complied. "What if we were married?"

"Are you proposing?"

"No, I'm asking. What if?"

"Then I suppose we'd be sitting right where we are tonight after getting one of those quickie Dominican divorces like your buddy Jane Fonda or somebody. What's the difference?" he asked. "Most marriages are mistakes. Unlikely ones, even the loveless ones, seem to turn out about as well as any. Hell with love."

"Now you don't believe in love?"

"Sure I do, backed with guts, luck, same philosophy of life, whatever you call what we don't have."

"We don't have?"

"You know, each doing our own thing even if neither of us wants it that way. We must be missing something."

"The boat probably."

He smiled slightly and his eyes softened. "Well, we talked about it once anyway. After that Puerto Plata thing. Remember?"

Remember? "Of course," she nodded. Some things were pivotal, too cherished to forget, ever. "It's not a memory even," she confessed. "It's part of who I am."

First always, she remembered the morning sun that day. White hot in the sky, singeing the green hills and blue water. An hour later braising her bare skin as the boat chugged north, peeling the sea.

The French divers crowded aft of them in the small rented bote, complaining loudly in their native tongue about the exorbitant price of the trip while she pretended not to understand and Jack's eyes on her so heavy he hardly remembered to blink. She drank him in that day too, away on holiday alone with him to the island's undeveloped north coast, a carefree dive without the responsibility of anyone else's good time only his own, and hers. "It's something to do with the morning light," he'd said at the hotel. "Your hair has amber in it."

Jack managed his dive shop all day, taught pool classes most evenings, and spent his weekends in the ocean doing checkout dives. His hair was usually matted, and he never seemed to get the salt out. This time together was a gift, and she was determined to make it memorable. Divers came from all over the world to dive with Jack Doubleday. A few weeks ago he rescued a pro-football lineman. Three hundred pounds of stupid, who had lied about his diving certification and presented a very well made fake ID. Then panicked at sixty feet and shot to the surface. Jack handled the emergency as he did most things underwater, with professionalism and perfect calm. Like it happened every day. Laura felt his calm, his assuredness, and always the security he exuded. A confident athlete who knows he will win, and she loved him even more underwater.

She'd hardly noticed, but sometime during their passage across that vast expanse of morning sea, the French had slipped from complaints to demands. The Dominican boatman's jaw had set and his mouth compressed to a tight line as he twisted the outboard throttle. Jack had his back to them, and had twice before rolled his eyes at their agitation.

"This is getting serious," she leaned forward and told him. "Our boatman's starting to look pissed."

"The French are assholes," Jack said loud enough to be heard clearly if any of them spoke English. "Tell them to shut up."

Before she could answer, one of the women, there were two couples, turned to Jack. "You have a problem?"

"No," Jack said. "You people seem to have the problem."

"Be happy," she said, pursing her lips as if addressing a spoiled child. "We are renegotiating the price. We are saving you money."

"I wasn't unhappy with the price," Jack said, barely twisted toward her. "Leave it alone."

"American," she said. "Always plenty of money."

She turned away, back to the group and the beleaguered boatman. Laura saw the Dominican spoke no French or English and the negotiations were being carried out in such poor Spanish she feared little was understood on either side. The boatman was young and his lack of English meant he probably dealt very little with foreigners, and was likely suspicious of them. His broad face, full of smiles on the dock, was tight now and brooding. She knew he was taking the attempt to cut the price personally, an insult perhaps to his abilities, or worse, his manhood.

She leaned across to Jack. "Stop this," she said.

"What can I do?"

"Tell them we'll pay the difference."

"Like hell!"

"I'll pay it then."

"No, you won't."

"Wait," she said, holding up a hand. "I guess they've agreed on a new price. Our boatman isn't happy but he's going along. These people are just trying to make a point, I think. Get their way. He's nodding and ignoring them. I still don't like it."

Jack smiled. "Quit worrying. If he gets violent, I'll put a stop to it right after he kills the first four."

"Maybe," she said laughing, "you could've been a diplomat after all."

"My Finnish blood," he said. "My mother was Finn remember."

"Finns are great diplomats I suppose?"

"The best," he said. "You should know that. Don't you remember what they did in the Middle East?"

"What?"

"The UN deal with the Israelis. I've told you this story a hundred times."

"No you haven't."

"It's the one I always tell when somebody teases me about being half Finn. Had this UN peacekeeping force down there, troops from a dozen countries in those silly baby blue helmets, getting themselves between the Israelis and the Palestinians. So a Finnish force is sent to defend this little village out in the desert somewhere. Bunch of Palestinian freedom fighters living in the town. Israeli army camped a couple miles away ready to pounce. One night they do. Israeli commander figures, you know, bunch of Finns, what they gonna do?

"Night, alone in the desert, all the Israelis got to do is get past the Finns. They face off. Israeli commander says, *Move out or we'll blow your heads off*. Finns are a stubborn bunch and stand their ground. Finally the Israelis level their weapons and it's the moment of truth. Just before they fire the Finnish commander tells his troops to lay down their arms. Everyone relaxes, then he turns to his unarmed men and says in Finnish, *Okay fellas, kick their asses*. So they walk over and beat hell out of the Israeli army."

She stuck her tongue out at him. "You make this stuff up."

"It's true. Finnish diplomat told me himself at a party."

"When are we going to get there?"

"Pretty soon," he said looking ahead. "Won't be able to see anything, you know, just a shallow bank in the sea about sixty feet deep. Nothing shows on the surface."

"So the boatman has to know his business."

"Not just finding it, which he's probably been doing all his life, out fishing, but maintaining contact with us while we're under, that's the trick. Bubbles tend to get lost in open ocean."

"How comforting."

He grinned. "Don't worry. Visibility is 150-feet or better. If he can't see us, we'll see him."

A few minutes later the boat slowed, circled, then stopped dead in the water, bobbing in the light chop. Laura leaned across the gunwale and spotted the white sand bottom more than sixty feet below. The water was melted glass. "What will we see?" she asked, without turning.

"Bigger critters, more of them than we're accustomed to seeing down south. Better corals. A chunk of gold or silver for all I know. They don't call them the *Silver Banks* for nothing, I guess."

"You're not kidding?"

"Not in the least," he said. "Every boatman on the coast has a story about finding a nugget or a chunk of silver rolled into a log by the sea."

"Why don't they all have new boats then?" she said, turning, thrusting her chin out at him.

"Demon rum," he said.

"That's where you get all these stories. In bars."

"Best place in the world for stories. Be surprised how many turn out to be true."

Behind him the French were busy suiting up. The woman who'd spoken to Jack was instructing the boatman on how to hold her tank so she could slip into the back pack. The sun seemed absorbed by the water, its blue depths taking on the light as if the source were at the bottom instead of overhead.

So as not to swamp the boat, they took turns squatting on the gunwale and allowing the weight of their tanks to pull them backwards into the sea. The French first, then she went ahead of Jack, who waited above until she'd righted herself in the water and inflated her horse collar. "Okay?" he asked. Snorkel in her mouth, she signaled and he dropped down beside her. The water was warm and the salty taste made her pucker the mouthpiece.

Jack was a methodical diver, ignoring the chop, the panorama below, concentrating on their equipment. Testing regulators again in the water, examining pressure gauges, holding the back of her head in both his hands to carefully examine her mask skirt and be certain not a single hair strayed inside the seal. The French were half way to the bottom when they finally followed them, the surface slipping away as she heaved a great sigh of contentment, more comfortable with Jack underwater than with anyone else above.

They descended in a slow free fall, spinning face down, knees bent, hands pressing the gentle passage of the water between their fingers, carefully examining the topographical view of the bank. Jack had an uncanny sense of direction and she knew before they settled on the sand he would know exactly where they were, and as they swam in zigzags, circles, and angles during the dive she would become confused, but he would not. In the end, he'd turn magically and point out the boat above, or the direction to swim to find it. Her confidence in him converted underwater delight into contentment. She removed her regulator and mouthed "I love you," but his eyes were searching out a landing site on a smooth patch of sand. It was okay that he didn't see her.

Years later she would remember that dive as the very best ever. Not for any great event - they found no gold or silver - but because the serenity of it planted itself in her memory and grew, shading her during the torrid or hectic times. After twenty years, thirty, she could conjure up that day with such clarity she'd taste salt on her lips and accept again the warm liquid embrace of the South Atlantic, the sand gently pricking her knees as she knelt watching the sea fans and schooling porgies, yellow goatfish, and bluestriped grunts.

They moved slowly. Held hands and let go and held hands again. The only sound was the rhythm of their breathing. The French disappeared almost immediately and she was glad to be rid of them. An hour passed in a wink, and yet, she felt as if she'd been underwater so long the dry world ceased to exist. Even then, at the very time it was happening, she knew somehow that these moments were destined to remain with her always. She wondered if this wasn't how one of her old Hebrew prophets felt as Jehovah whispered truth in his ear, nourished and enlightened but powerless to share it with those who knew it not. So she decided then to keep it all to herself. A forever perfect hour.

Now, with their pressure gauges reading less than 500 pounds, Jack knelt on the sand scanning the reef clusters and beds of soft corals for the other diver's bubble trails until finally he shrugged and started them back in the direction of the boat.

Minutes later she knew they were in trouble. Jack formed the bow of a boat with his hands and shrugged. It wasn't visible anywhere. They did finally spot the thrashing legs of the French divers clustered on the surface. She saw resignation in Jack's magnified eyes. He signaled reluctantly for her to begin the ascent.

On the surface there was a commotion. The French screaming, one of the women close to hysterics. The men swearing the most foul oaths, gesturing in the direction of the distant coast. Jack's head rose slowly and he said nothing, only spit out his regulator mouthpiece and made the OK sign to her. After she responded he turned to face the others.

"The boat's gone," he said, not asking.

"Yes!" the woman who spoke English shouted. "The fool. Coward!"

"A fool," Jack said quietly, "is someone niggardly, nine miles from shore. He won't be back. Hope you're good swimmers."

"He will not dare to leave us here."

"Do you see a boat? It's mid-day. They'll be having their siesta back on shore. Our little boatman, later this afternoon in his favorite bar, will amuse his friends with a story about how he got even," he growled, barely kicking to keep his chin above water. "We'll still be swimming."

One of the men said something she couldn't catch and the woman translated. "He will be dead when we get back."

"If," Jack told her. "If we get back."

The French were all for sitting it out on the surface until more fishing boats happened along in search of an afternoon catch on the banks. Jack explained that fishing was done mostly in the early morning and again in late afternoon. Were they willing to risk being found at five or six o'clock? And if not, to spend the night in open sea? Better to swim and hope for the best. If no one came before dark at least they'd be closer to shore.

"What time is it dark?" asked the woman.

"Seven, seven-thirty."

"We would not be to land by then?"

"Open ocean. Might swim a mile every hour or so without all this equipment, no current, calm seas, a compass to steer by, no cramps. Luck." He shrugged. "Might make it by ten if the sharks don't feed on us."

The woman's face, already pale, blanched. She turned and conveyed this to her companions in short bursts. They were all tiring now from treading water instead of resting back in their horse collars as she and Jack had done.

Laura knew Jack was only annoyed, not frightened, and she quietly asked, "Can we really swim nine miles?"

"If you can swim a mile you can swim a hundred. Anyway, we're not swimming, we're snorkeling. It's gentler even than walking, and easier. We won't use our arms, just paddle, pace ourselves, rest when we want, then back at it." He placed both hands inside his flotation collar and lowered it away from his chin. "I might've been a little optimistic with the Frenchys. Closer to midnight probably before we get there, but we'll make it, don't worry."

"I'm not, as long as you're right beside me."

"That's exactly where I'm going to be," he said. "Except when I'm tired and you have to push me."

The French woman swam back to them again, clumsily, Laura thought, and they listened to the latest committee decision. "We cannot swim with the equipment," she told them.

"It won't be easy," Jack answered. "I think we should wear it awhile though, just in case we need to go under for any reason. Tanks will keep the afternoon sun off our backs, too. We can always ditch it later."

"Do as you wish," she said and returned to the others who had already loosened their back packs, allowing the near empty steel cylinders to drift slowly toward the reef below.

To Laura, Jack said, "Play with your buoyancy until it's perfect. Until you can't feel the tank. You'll be comfortable with it after a bit. They're nearly empty, almost neutral. We used to swim out from shore on the surface a mile or two easily, dive, then swim back again. Tanks give us one more option, we can go down, at least for awhile. More options are usually better than less." He smiled. "Or maybe I don't have the slightest idea what I'm talking about."

So they prepared themselves. Jack had explained to the French that the current, though slight, was predominately westerly and slightly off shore, northwesterly sometimes. He wanted to angle east a bit. They reluctantly agreed to follow, if, as one man pointed out, Jack could swim in a straight line.

If she hadn't been young or a strong swimmer or out there with Jack, Laura might've been scared. She wasn't. Just uneasy, cautious about the next few hours. All of it tempered with a kind of fierce excitement like the tension before a race in which she knew she'd excel if she kept focus and didn't make mistakes. Nine miles from land in the open sea their position was precarious regardless of Jack's bravado, or even his experience. A hundred things could go wrong. The sea was no one's mistress. Earth's most savage creatures lived there still, against all odds. This was a day, a night, none of them would forget.

Jack had rules, and lectured them before they started. The real test, he'd said, came almost immediately. Once they left the relatively shallow water of the banks the ocean floor dropped off to more than 4,000 fathoms, almost 25,000 feet - five miles deep. You wouldn't see the sea fans. Nothing but blue water until they reached the coast. Nothing to guide them. At the beginning they'd swim single file so each diver had the person in front to follow. He cautioned them to spend more time looking at the fins ahead than the depths below. Later, he believed they could swim side by side awhile holding hands. Gets lonely, he told them. It was a strange kind of thing for Jack to say, she thought.

His other rules were about maintaining contact, resting, pacing themselves; avoiding exhaustion, hyperventilation, and panic at all costs. Their worst enemies would be themselves. The sea, he said, may do nothing at all, just lie there and let them swim through it. They could drown or not, as they saw fit. Or it might rise up and do everything in its power to destroy them, and in that event, he thought it would probably be successful. It rested with them to be careful. Avoid dumb mistakes. Take no chances. And most of all, he repeated, not to make themselves tired no matter how long it took for the swim.

An hour later Laura realized he'd forgotten the most important warning - boredom. She played with the air volume in her BC until it was so perfect the tank hardly existed, then she played with it again and again until her snorkel dug into the water and she choked. She counted kick cycles all the way to two thousand, got tired of it, switched to varying her following distance from Jack's fins. She'd thrust forward, lag, thrust again and coast, stay even, pound the water with her fins. Lagging too far, she struck the Frenchman behind in the face with a fin blade. After that she went back to a steady stroke.

The first couple hours Jack stopped nearly every fifteen minutes to count heads and give everyone a moment to rest and regroup. This annoyed the French. They were without equipment now except their masks, fins, and snorkels and very macho, even the women, eager to swim hard without stopping. Jack gradually agreed to fewer stops, gaining confidence in them as they swam. She was glad too, because when they stopped and brought their heads up she could see the coastline, a dark wrinkle on the distant horizon, and it was no closer then before. After two hours shouldn't they have covered two miles? Wasn't two miles roughly twenty-something percent of the total distance to shore? Why wasn't it any closer? Why did the land move out ahead of them? Without the mountains she wasn't even sure they'd see land at all. What if Jack was wrong about the currents? What if they just swam forever and came no nearer?

These worries suddenly seemed trivial when they plowed into a school of jellyfish. Acres of them. She wasn't frightened at first, not until she saw the larger ones with tentacles hanging down 20 or 30 feet, like spidery legs dancing in the current. She hoped they weren't Portuguese man-of-war, close kin to the jellyfish but along its tentacles are stinging cells of the most toxic poison. Small jellyfish administer little more than a zing, but the man-of-war, with its long deadly tentacles, can cause major paralysis. Human organs cease to function. A tentacle, even after it's separated from the man-of-war's body and cast up on a beach miles away, still retains enough potency to cause excruciating pain to an unwary beachcomber. They were soon surrounded by hundreds of jellyfish.

The translucent creatures drift helplessly with the currents, unable to maneuver. They covered a large area and she saw tops of bells down almost as far as she dared look. She worried Jack might stop, curious as to how they were making it behind him. If their legs dropped down into the field of jellyfish, they were sure to be stung. She swam closer, almost into his fin wash.

Minutes later she realized she hadn't come near a jellyfish and craned her neck to watch Jack. Calmly, almost offhandedly, he was clearing the field ahead. His hands moved out, touched a jellyfish bell, then deftly flipped it away a couple feet as he swam forward at almost the same speed they'd made before chancing into the field. She saw him flip one jellyfish away with his left hand while simultaneously picking another by the bell and tossing it above his head where it landed more than a yard to the right with a silent splash. Not only wasn't he panicked, she wasn't sure he even considered the jellyfish. They might just as well have been an acre of bubbles in his path. She was relieved to see he gave the larger ones a wide berth.

Sometime later they reached clear water without a sting, still on course. "Jack, you old salt," she said into her snorkel and turned to see if the French were impressed. They had gone.

Laura pushed hard against the water with her fins and felt the strain in her upper leg muscles as she pulled alongside Jack and brought him to a halt. "We lost them," she said breathlessly.

Huffing manually to save air, Jack inflated his horse collar BC until the relief valve burped. The black device, slick with sea water, lifted him by the crotch and he gained maximum height in the water. She followed suit, eyes flicking nervously in all directions, but the French had disappeared. "They couldn't have panicked and drown back there?" she asked, dealing first with the worst possibility.

"Not all four." He sounded tired.

"Where are they?"

Jack moved in a slow circle before answering, scanning 360-degrees. "If they went around the jellyfish field, turning right to move with the current, which they've wanted to do all along, then they must be somewhere to the west. Maybe a quarter mile or more away by now. I suppose we need to go after them."

"What if you're wrong and they went the other way?"

Jack extended the rubber inflator hose above his head and air hissed free. Lying back, he rested his head on the softened collar and bobbed peacefully in the chop. "There's a point of land, Cabo Frances Viejo, see it on the horizon? That's where we *were* going. West is the bay between Rio San Juan and Sosua. Cuts in quite a ways. Can't see across it from here. A much, much longer swim. We miss the Cabo now we'll have to swim against the current to go back, or add another six or seven miles to the swim. Those arrogant bastards have just screwed themselves. Us too."

The water temperature was 82-degrees and Laura shivered suddenly, so cold her teeth rattled. "Why can't we see them?" On her back, she paddled until she was alongside him and felt the length of his body against hers, drawing warmth from his upper leg and buttocks.

"Up high on a boat or ship you got maybe a 12 mile line of sight to the horizon. In the water you're almost blind, like trying to see the whole prairie from a gopher hole."

"So they could be closer than we think?"

"Maybe."

"Hadn't we better be looking?"

"I'm thinking," he said.

"About?"

"If they did do something smart for once and go left, and we go right...." he allowed the thought to dangle.

She knew if they swam away from them that was it. They'd see them on shore, or never. Sunshine warmed her face. If they had time, she'd slip the mask off awhile and let it soak in. "I'm a coward," she muttered, water lapping her cheeks. "I want you to decide about the French, about everything."

"What?"

"Nothing."

Jack straightened himself in the water and air hissed from his BC. "If there's one thing we can depend on it's arrogance," he said. "Gets the best of good judgment every time. They went right."

For the better part of an hour they swam hard on a southwesterly course where Jack hoped to intercept them. She was relieved and slightly winded when he stopped suddenly and kicked himself high in the water to see ahead. "There," he pointed, and she saw clearly an orange snorkel tip cresting a wave. They were alive at least.

Their reunion was not joyful. They blamed Jack for first leading them into a jellyfish field and then abandoning them. He and Laura were invited to join the group or swim alone as they wished, but no one was in a mood to follow Jack anywhere. He was undependable. That was their word, undependable, and for the first time she spoke to them in their own language and told them point blank that if they had followed closely and not panicked they would be a mile closer to shore now instead of having added who knows how many miles and hours to the swim. Her undiplomatic speech was interrupted by Jack, who ran his hand gently along her rib cage underwater, and said aloud, "Okay. We'll follow you."

When all four had their heads in the water swimming away, she asked, "What's the matter with you? They don't know what they're doing!"

"I know." He exhaled slowly and she noticed beads of sweat on his forehead inside the mask. "Can we leave them? They're like 16-year-olds with new driving licenses, too dumb to know the danger they're in."

"They got us into this mess and now won't let us get them out," she complained, growing more angry as she spoke, spitting against the salt water. "They aren't dumb. They're pricks. Just pricks!"

Jack threw his head back and laughed. His voice carried out across the water and with the flat of her hand she splashed him until her arm ached and he swam alongside and tried to kiss her and their masks collided.

The afternoon sun forced itself into the pores of her exposed flesh as they swam on again. She felt it even through her hair, on the back of her neck and shoulders where the backpack couldn't protect her. The rays hurt but didn't warm her. She was thankful for the tank now, saving her back. They swam slower with the tanks, not from weight, but drag, working hard as minutes and hours slipped away. They concentrated on swimming, closing the distance between themselves and the other four who kept up an admirable pace with nothing to slow them but the passage of water along their slick bodies.

It was right, what Jack said about swimming, and she'd lost count of such trivialities as miles. The aching in her upper legs and along the center of her back had dulled to a kind of deep soreness she overcame with effort and stubbornness. She'd developed only one cramp, oddly in the arch of her foot, and relieved it by grabbing her fin blade and pulling back until the muscle stretched and loosened the knot. She took silent pride in her body. Her mind was another matter.

This was the kind of thing, she knew, rarely experienced by someone like her. It simply wasn't permitted. Her father's diplomatic career, though slow to get started, had blossomed after marriage to her mother, and money. Theirs was an intellectual home, and a kind one. Laura's older brother, John Alan, left home for Yale in '69, then on to medical school, residency, settling finally in Portland. When he turned his back on the Foreign Service it fell to her - short, blunt, literary, and female. Somehow, the family bore up under the strain, patiently. Her assignment first to Quito, Ecuador and then the Dominican Republic, was a family disappointment. She embraced it. The Latino atmosphere was more festive and the people loved to dress up.

The best thing about the 70s was long dresses. They hid her high heels and gave her as much height as she could safely strap to her feet. Stilts, had they been stylish. Slightly splayfooted, she'd become a daredevil in heels and wouldn't be caught dead in sneakers and jeans. She wore spikes so high they had to be custom made, and in causal clothes high heeled sandals with thick soles. She'd danced the twist and won a limbo contest in spikes, and made it look easy. She could drink straight bourbon for four hours and converse knowledgeably on a myriad of subjects and do it fluently in four languages. Today she was swimming the Atlantic

Ocean - 25,000 feet deep and miles from land. It didn't even seem incredible.

In one fluid motion, Jack slowed and backed in beside her like an expert parallel-parker. He took her hand and they swam on. There were things in the water she'd never noticed before - waves of plankton, silver sardines in swirling counter-clockwise schools that caught the sunlight and hurt her eyes, large numbers of flying fish, bits of grass, a plastic bottle, and small slicks of bilge oil. No large animals. She remembered hearing someone say that there was one shark for every square mile of ocean and that meant they should encounter close to a dozen on this course. She held her breath, ducked her head underwater and stared back between her legs at the blind spot behind them.

Laura had no great fear of sharks, less she thought than Jack, and had swam with both sand sharks and the more docile nurse. But she didn't relish a large hammerhead or even a swift mako coming up hungry from the depths to investigate their splashing. Between her legs she saw nothing but blue behind them, but when the sun was gone and darkness hid the deep she worried each stroke of their fins would send signals through acres and acres of ocean, a call to dine. There was no chance now they could reach land before nightfall.

A tight and urgent squeeze of her hand and she snapped her head around and saw Jack pointing slightly ahead and below. She cleared water from her snorkel and breathed in sharply. Far below, a line of spotted eagle rays the size of Volkswagens feathered their wings and flew silently, sunlight flickering along their broad bodies. Their sudden appearance allayed her fears and she returned Jack's squeeze, smiling so broadly sea water gathered inside her lip.

The rays were a good omen, swimming toward the shallower reefs of the island to feed. She poked Jack for the time. Almost 4:30. How often had she snorkeled from shore to watch the large rays feeding in the shallows? Was this so different? They'd just be a little later getting home was all.

Sunset doesn't linger in tropical latitudes and the sky, domed above the earth, provides a brief twilight peek at the glories of heaven, and disappears. Night truly falls, and hours of daylight and dark are relatively even, as March or October in the north. With the sun setting in Haiti on the island's western expanse, Jack swam out ahead of the French and stopped them. They clustered, treading water.

"Half an hour and it'll be dark," Jack addressed them. "Sosua is around the point to our right, I hope, but we won't see any lights for quite awhile. Rio San Juan is to the left, maybe, but it's tiny and few homes have electricity. We may not see a single light. Have you thought about how we'll stick together? How we'll navigate?"

Laura, not content to let the French woman translate, did it herself, emphasizing what she knew from experience, that it was as easy to swim in circles as it was to walk in them if you didn't have a good point of reference.

When the discussion ended, the woman turned to Laura and said, "We are not to follow this man." She nodded at Jack.

Jack got the message. "On the boat," he said, "in my dive bag, is my compass. Instead of sticking it in my BC pocket, I suffered from overconfidence. Don't want to follow me, okay, but look behind you. That's a squall line. Maybe fifteen or twenty miles wide and a foot deep, or one hell of storm that'll last hours. Ocean does what it does, my overconfidence, or yours, won't have any effect on it, only on our lives. Imagine a pounding rain at dark, no way to stay together, wind, waves whipped up to eight, nine feet or more. We work together or there's a good chance we'll die together. Follow that?"

Like the rest, Laura hadn't seen the black bank of clouds on the northeastern horizon behind them and she fumbled through the translation and was rescued by the French woman who gave a faithful account of Jack's warning.

They wanted to know, what did the American suggest?

"I've been thinking about it for over an hour," he said. "At first the clouds looked pretty flat but they've been moving too fast, building up too high for anything small. In the dark, in heavy seas, I don't think six people can stay close even if we had rope to tie ourselves together. We're three couples and I think we're best looking after each other that way. Laura and I still have our weight belts. We'll fastened them together to make a lifeline. You've each got BCs with long crotch straps. Take them apart and clip them together, tied to your wrists if necessary." Jack popped his mask off, swept his hair back and ran his hand across his face. "When it gets light we might be able to get back together. If not, we swim for shore two by two. At least we're not alone."

Laura rested back in the warm water and ignored the discussion in French. She'd take her chances with Jack and it was all she needed to hear. He'd decided for her. Not asking her advice. Undoubtedly never considering it. Why wasn't she offended? The sunset yellowed the broken clouds gathered over the land, greened the sky and highlighted the boiling storm clouds behind them in such a soft white as to make them benign. She wasn't offended by Jack's peremptoriness because they were of one mind, like old married folks reading each other's thoughts. A notion that brought a smile to her salty lips. She felt them crack and tasted sweet blood.

If he asked her to marry him this minute, she'd say yes without a second thought. Not the smoothest man she'd met, but fearless. No. It wasn't fearlessness but the acceptance of risk. Jack sanctioned danger as the price for breathing, unlike her father, who let money rob him of risk, so life was safe, comfortable, secure. She knew then that her parents bought their security by surrendering the uncertainty that gives life its kick. Jack was incapable of such precaution, and she feared he was also incapable of such security. Life with Jack would always be a long swim in open water.

"Hey shorty! Wake up!"

"Be quiet, and don't call me that."

"Then pay attention," he commanded. "I'm going to slip your weight belt off and you hold the weights while I get mine off and buckle the two together, then I'll help you get the weights on the waist band strap for your backpack. Simple. Just don't drop anything."

"What'd the others say?" she asked, refusing to cut short her rest.

"Still gabbing."

"Why can't we take a two-hour nap? I can sleep just like this and while we're sleeping the storm will blow over and the stars will come out and you will navigate us to shore in time for a late dinner."

"Idiot," he said. "Mason isn't French is it?"

"I can French kiss."

"Hold these," he said, piling the two, three-pound pieces of lead on her chest just above her breasts. "Work first. Look back there. That thing's a monster, black and wide. The sea'll be whipped up for miles. We're going to tie ourselves together and let that bastard blow us ashore."

"Can that work?"

"Probably not, but I like to think about it."

"I like to think about clean smooth sheets and a shower. Do you have any idea what this salt is doing to my skin?"

"Your lips are puffy and cracked. Some red blotches on your cheeks. Hair's kind of crusty. All in all, no worse than any other bit of flotsam and jetsam." He grinned at her and she saw his own lips crack. "If you wash up on a beach after the storm nobody's gonna be in a big hurry to carry you off."

"Well," she said, "for a moment there I thought you weren't going to try and comfort me before we have to swim for our lives."

A moment later the French agreed to the plan but were convinced they'd have no trouble staying together. They took the lead again and Laura's leg muscles ached as she put pressure on them and high up in her buttocks a deep soreness forced a gasp from her lips.

What can waves do to us she wondered? Raise us and lower us? Somersault us? Pelt us with salted spray? And rain? We're as wet as we can get, and a refreshing drink of rain water would go down nicely. Almost submerged, like submarines at the surface, she felt a part of the water. Odd, being curious about her own suffering, like wondering what it's like to fall from a great height, almost wanting it.

Over her shoulder the storm crept up slowly, and the nearer it came the more it seemed to blur, losing its ferocious appearance. No longer a hard black wall but a soft gray bank of rain. The vast Atlantic that had stretched out behind them, a frightful void, was cloaked now by the intimacy of the storm, narrowing their world to a smaller, more manageable stage on which they could perform easily.

Without warning the sea began to flap before the wind. Light chop replaced by sharp, quick waves that rose to half a man's height and struck, one after another, with barely a trough between. Before long her body lifted and fell, jarred by the strap securing her to Jack. She looked for him. He was above, then below, above again. They collided, tanks ringing as metal struck metal. She saw his helplessness and it only clarified her own. No way to speak to him. Every part of her focused on the next wave and the next and the next.

Seas increased rapidly in size and a gray bank of rain bore down and pounded against the water, driving millions of humming drops into the torn surface, making a froth of it, then carrying it away before the wind. It tore at her face and she feared the loss of her mask. She knew survival without it was hopeless, and fumbled to tighten the strap with one hand as she fought against the water with the other. She tumbled and the lifeline snapped taut, wrenching her back, squeezing a panicked breath from her lungs.

Then Jack was there, grabbing the collar of her BC in both hands and shouting, "Deflate your BC!" before spinning away on his back.

Could he have meant inflate instead of deflate? Why would he say deflate? They would sink. Sink below the waves. Breath fresh, dry air from the tanks.

She saw him close again holding his regulator aloft so she would understand. She nodded emphatically, groping behind her for the hose and second stage. It had disappeared. Systematically, ignoring the savage blows of the water, she felt first along the right side of her body, then along the tank, in the crevice between body and tank. Could it have flipped over the tank? She held her breath, closed her eyes and tried to quiet her heart as she pushed the tank up with her left hand and reached back to find the valve with her right. The first stage of the regulator was fastened securely to the valve. No amount of sea water could dislodged a brass fitting locked in place by high pressure air. If she located the valve she could feel the hose and follow it to the second stage mouthpiece.

The hose was looped, twisted by the water and the rolling of her body, but she slid her hand along it until finally it straightened and she held it firmly. Jack waved and they stuffed the mouthpieces into their mouths and descended.

At first there was little relief and she equalized twice before the roiling water settled down enough for her to make out Jack signaling OK and she could see the bottoms of the waves marching overhead. When she answered, he signaled for her to slow her breathing, to relax and conserve air. Their tanks were nearly empty. Fifteen minutes or even less breathing time. A rest at least.

On the surface she'd been too frightened to notice the water motion, but here, where it moved more rhythmically, her stomach tightened against wave after wave of nausea. Jack had already leveled off and was swimming, leading her, studying his depth gauge to maintain as shallow a position as possible to conserve air but avoid the worst of the wave action. She desperately wanted to stop him and explain about the nausea but maybe it would go away after she swam awhile.

Almost without warning she felt bile rise at the back of her throat, her stomach soured, her shoulders contracted and vomit spewed from her mouth into the regulator mouthpiece. She bit down hard but the force of the discharge separated the rubber mouthpiece from the regulator second stage and when Laura inhaled, seawater rushed in and she swallowed it, causing her to vomit again.

Recognizing her peril she allowed the vomit to eject and grabbing the regulator without its mouthpiece, jammed it between her lips and inhaled wildly. Air flowed again into her lungs. She repeated this process several times until her stomach settled down and the retching stopped. The rubber mouthpiece was gone and she was now forced to suck the chrome-plated brass of the second stage itself, oily and metallic. Jack missed her struggle completely, irritated at having to pull her along on the lifeline. She pointed to her mouth and he came closer, only then noticing the solid bits of vomitus surrounding them in the water.

He nodded and blinked his eyes slowly to offer sympathy. She shrugged an apology, and they swam on.

Jack was able now to swim close to her and hold her wrinkled hand in his and when she pointed to their bleached, prunish skin, he only made his hand into a claw and shook it in her face and growled. Why am I laughing, she thought?

They moved slowly at a depth between twenty-five and thirty feet and Jack referred to the depth gauge often, and by watching the surface, seemed able to navigate in a straight line. But what is a straight line in the water? Circles would've seemed just as straight, or figure eights. She depended on him totally now and each time she glanced at her pressure gauge it seemed she'd sucked up another fifty pounds. How long could they stay down?

Minutes later she had an answer. It grew dark and they were forced to surface.

It didn't seem they'd been down long but the leading edge of the storm had passed, leaving behind larger seas and heavy rains but the waves were less ragged and lifted them more gently. Visibility was down to barely a block and they wallowed along in the heart of the squall, waiting for total darkness.

Jack wasted no time in getting them back on snorkel and swimming again, taking advantage of the storm to move them closer to shore. He didn't speak to her until all light had faded and they were lost in an inky blackness so complete the steady rain seemed a surprise with each drop that struck her face or hair. "How are you holding up?" he asked, his voice heavy and far away in the rain.

"I'm cold."

"It takes awhile to catch a chill in water this warm," he said. "Happens, though. Keep swimming. Keep the heart rate up."

"We're not going to die or anything, are we?"

"Not tonight," he said. "If we're still swimming in the morning and this thing blows off and we don't see land, I'll probably change my mind."

"Has to be land somewhere."

"Cuba, Puerto Rico or Great Britain, depending on which way we're headed. Unless I'm right." She felt the smile when he asked, "Sure you're not French?"

"I wonder where they are."

He grunted. "Body surfed like a pod of porpoise. On shore already. Griping to some bartender about the price of Brugal and Coca Cola."

"Wouldn't they be searching for us instead?"

"In a pig's eye."

This response quieted her. He wasn't depending on anyone but himself. Good to know. She'd known all along of course, but it didn't hurt to hear it. Not at all.

They swam on.

Rain managed to find a way down her snorkel tube, at first annoying, then refreshing as she ran it around inside her mouth, swallowing. Soft water, not cool as she'd have liked. She imagined a tall glass of Brugal on ice, Monolito pouring a rippling stream of Coca Cola gently to top it. A thick wedge of lime, swollen with juice to cut its sweetness. She listened to it fizz. What was Jack thinking, keeping her out here half the night when she needed a drink?

"I'm mad at you," she said into the tube and a drop of rainwater wetted her tongue.

Then came the worst time for her, the monotony of swimming on and on, struggling to concentrate, fasten herself in the void. Swimming on in a black liquid place that seemed to her intimate and vast, sloshing in its bowels, an endless beast that breasted on through an endless night, neither digesting her nor spitting her out, imprisoned forever in formless, liquid purgatory. The lifeline tugged her gently, reminding her to swim ahead, to push her fin blades against the water, keep her arms tucked along her body, head at a proper angle so the snorkel didn't dip seawater, inhale cautiously, exhale sharply, draw a fresh breath of sweet air. Disregard the drag of the tank on her back. Concentrate. Push the water.

If she'd been asked when the storm ended, she could not have said. It ended. Jack slowed her to a stop almost as if he were easing down a runaway horse. "Let's rest a minute," he said.

Except for the southern sky, stars beamed from the heavens, a prism field of sharp light that fell into the sea and was absorbed as if it had fallen into deep black carpet. "I didn't know it stopped raining," she said, and stared a long time in the direction the land had been. "There's no light."

"Storm's ashore now. It'll hang in the coastal mountains awhile before it moves on." He pulled her to him with the lifeline. "We'll see a shore light in a couple hours. Still a long swim."

"The others?" She could just make out an outline of his head and shoulders against the sparkling sky.

"Gone."

"God bless them," she said.

"Yes," Jack answered quietly. "If He can find them."

"What now?"

"Swim."

"What time is it?"

"Close to midnight."

"How much more?"

"Morning, I suppose, if we're lucky."

His voice sounded tired and she wished to see his face, read its lines. Was the jaw tight, or did it sag in defeat? Would he hide the truth from her in the dark? "I don't want to swim anymore if we can't make it." She didn't have the will to cry. "I can't work that hard unless you're sure."

Closer still until both his hands cradled her head and tilted it toward him. Their masks bumped. "I'm sure," he said.

"I want to look at you."

"I'm so sure, that if you swim steady for the next few hours I'll marry you."

She considered this awhile and said, "Seems to me like you win both ways on that deal."

"Obviously," he admitted. "If I marry you it means I lived, and if I died, I got to stay a bachelor for what was left of my life."

"Men," she said.

They swam on. She never knew where the strength came from or how her legs pumped all those miles with only one cramp in her foot, or what thing inside her powered the hope that kept the heart and legs pumping. She later told the story at a hundred cocktail parties until she wondered if she hadn't made it all up. But there was no way, really, to tell about that night. The hours and hours of aching muscles, or the fear and uncertainty, the loneliness of being lost on a black sea, every decision a guess, every stroke an assumption. How can that be condensed into polite chat? So she made of it a kind of joke. The rest she carried hidden in her heart.

It wasn't even swimming, really. It was waiting. Waiting for the squall to move over the mountains. Waiting for a light. Then waiting longer to be certain of it. Not to fool yourself because there were lights in your head sometimes, and lights in circles around your eyes and lights in the sky, some that glided and some that only winked.

Once a sound like bawling cattle rose from the deep and stood up the hair on her arms and sent shivers along her spine. When she first heard it she pretended it was nothing, a sound from somewhere inside herself. The feeling she got that it was being transmitted by the water in sonic waves, striking her skin, was imagination, fatigue. It wasn't until her skin prickled with it, her salt encrusted skull crawled with it, that she stopped Jack and begged him to make it go away.

"Whales," he said, and she didn't believe him. Something else. Ghost riders in the sky.

The sunrise - finally. Indigo to orange, fading to the palest yellow, strengthening and strengthening until it burst from the sea, relighting water and land, and the land was green and not a blur, clear enough to distinguish clumps of palms on a small beach to their left and high cliffs along most of the coastline, white water at their feet. She turned without a word and swam steadily for the sandy beach.

If Jack hadn't pulled the lifeline she would've swam and swam until there was no more water under her and then crawled along the sand and buried her face in its warmth. "Wait," he said sharply. "We can't go through the surf with the lifelines."

His face was pocked with wounds and inside the mask his eyelashes hung heavy with salt. The soreness of his swollen lips must match her own as she tried to speak. "Don't leave me now."

"We'll get all tangled up." He flipped open the quick release and freed the buckle. "Inflate your BC and let the waves ride you ashore. Don't stand up. Crawl until you reach dry sand. Use the regulator. There's enough air left. Just enough."

"God, you're bossy." She tried not to smile and break her skin. "This what I've got to look forward to after we're married?"

"We're not on shore yet. The breakers are bigger than they look. Hold the regulator in your mouth. Keep swimming. Inflate now and go. I'll be right behind you."

It was the easiest part, a water ride. She scratched a knee on some coral, her only injury except the damage done her skin. The coral cut infected later because she ignored it, and the scar she carried as a lifelong reminder of the day, and the swim, which turned out near as they could reconstruct to be a few yards above 12 miles - half the distance across the English Channel, an impossible feat for all but the best of swimmers.

They teased each other about the marriage proposal all the remainder of that day as they napped and rested, tending their skin sores and cracked lips with salves bought at a local farmacia. Later, still exhausted, they searched the scattered local cafes and bars for the French.

That evening a bartender told them their boatman had gone to visit his sister in a remote mountain village after some French tourists raised all manner of hell in the Police hut at Sosua. One of the women had a broken wrist which occurred because she was tied to her partner by an American whom she sincerely hoped had perished in the sea. As Laura translated this tale to Jack he was seized with laughter and his lips opened again, bleeding so freely the bartender was forced to dab them with a paper napkin.

By nine o'clock, too tipsy to eat, they went back to the hotel and slept in a bed that sloshed them side to side until morning. Neither of them ever mentioned getting married again, forsaking the idea somewhere out there on the ocean, lover's flotsam.

Now it wasn't fit dinner conversation. Even at the end.

The caged yellow mechanical bird sat on its trapeze, swinging in repetitive rhythm, the perpetual cadence of the inanimate. The music played, competing with local rhythms from the bar, and the bird did a sort of bow intended to keep time with the beat of the songs. Tonight Laura was captivated by the bird's mechanical motion, counting to herself the number of times it caught the beat.

"Did you hear what I said?" Jack asked. "About the Puerto Plata thing?"

"Yes. I heard what you said about marriage too."

"I just meant that was our chance," he said. "And we didn't take it."

"I heard you."

"Well?"

"Well what?"

"You're just bound and determined to make this difficult aren't you?"

She sighed and turned from the bird. "You bring up marriage again at the eleventh hour. What's the point? We survived Puerto Plata. We'd never survive marriage."

"I just wanted to remind you that we've been through all that."

"Thank you," she said politely. "I need to be reminded."

"Sorry," Jack told her, lowering his menu. Magically, Monolito appeared at her elbow. "He must have radar or something," Jack said, holding up his empty glass, then pointing at Laura's. "Two mas."

"Ahhh!" Monolito exclaimed, wide-eyed. "You speaka the Espanish!"

"Right," Jack said. "I'm really catching on to the lingo."

"I just want to say one more thing." Laura waited for Monolito to remove himself. "Then I'll be quiet, eat dinner and play out the rest of the scene."

Jack frowned, relit his cigar.

"Listen to me, Jack." She waited for his eyes. "No matter what happens, who goes or stays, I love you." She paused. "Understand? I don't want anyone else but you."

He used the lighter she'd bought him at Christmas. "I know."

"I'll tell you something else," she said. "You're no better off. It's me for you too."

His face softened. The cigar was shoved to the corner of his mouth and when he spoke his voice seemed richer. "You're incredible." He didn't avoid her eyes. "You *are* exactly what I want."

Monolito put their drinks down. "Muy bien," he said, and departed.

"We're in the wrong place at the wrong time, Laura," he began again. "I'm scared to death I can't live without you."

"Jack."

"Let me finish." He held up his hand. "Women always think they're authorities on love. You had me ten minutes after I met you." He pressed a finger into his drink and stirred slowly. "Trouble is, we'd end up hating each other."

There was an uneasiness in Laura's stomach. "Don't say that," she muttered. "Even if it's true."

"Truth is whatever we choose to remember," he said. Blue smoke hung in the air above his head. "And it's enough."

"Just enough," she answered. "I'm hungry." Laura had never been so hungry. "I'm going to cry," she said. But she didn't. She was too happy, and too sad.

"Why don't you order the grilled ham you like so much?" Jack said. "With the pineapple ring on top."

"Yes," she said. "I think I will."

Later that night, she did kiss Jack. Right there in the cafe in front of everybody. Monolito cried.

Much later when he cleared their table and switched the lights off for the night, he returned the sign to its place there on a fresh white tablecloth - "Reservado." Weeks and weeks went by before he knew the Americans would never return. The waiters talked about them for awhile because it was a mystery, and they wondered.

She'd been sitting too long on the edge of the planter. Her fresh skirt was filthy. She got up so as not to crick her back. An old

Mercedes cab-over struggled to the diesel pump and blew a load of black smoke from its single stack. The noise and oily cloud annoyed her. There wouldn't be a taxi, not here. She beat the back of her skirt with one hand, then the other, and strolled again to the cafe windows to assess the damage.

She fought a sudden impulse to go around back and climb onto the roof. Jack had taken her there once long ago when he installed a lighted sign for his shop. When the work was finished they'd lingered in each other's arms until orange twilight fired the western sky and warmed their faces. She wondered, was the ocean still visible from there? The single story strip mall was surrounded now by tall apartment and office buildings, their rooftops littered with satellite dishes.

In the opaque window she saw the skirt was brushed clean. It was getting dark and she thought about having a drink somewhere before an evening underground in the Mesón de la Cava. The rocks and cool rooms of the cave didn't appeal to her now. She wanted to see a long way off, study a dark horizon, pinpoint the lights of ships. Several places on the Malecón might do, if she found a cab.

The meat market deli was still open. They'd have a phone.

How odd is the manner in which we worship our own history, Laura mused. Megan had been wrong about taking the past so lightly. It was, after all, the only safe place. You aren't forced to repeat your mistakes, or even own up to them. You couldn't change anything, but with a twist or two you might revise it just enough so it didn't hurt. Not in the least. And truth is whatever you remember.

She wondered though, as she walked toward the brash lights of the meat market, what happened to Jack Doubleday. She'd pined for him most of that year he left, but the earth swallowed him and she never heard his name again, not ever. How was it a person could disappear like that? Maybe he was dead. Maybe he had email.

A buzzer sounded far back in the shop as she opened the door.

Jimmy Olsen

The Hero
of Blind Pig Island

The boat drifted and the boy squinted into the old man's left eye.
"I can't see anything in it, Grandpa," he said.

"Okay." The old man leaned back. "Bit of sand I think. When we
get ashore I'll flush it with lake water."

"It's red though, and kind of weepy like."

The boy had a broad face with extraordinary dark eyelashes and a
head of near black hair, seldom combed. His brown eyes continued
to squint with concern. The old man smiled. "Rheumy they call it."

"What's rheumy?"

"Like weepy."

"Sounds worse."

"Don't fuss." Grandpa swung his seat back to face the steering
console and engaged the engine. "Let's get this little craft on the
beach and have a swim."

The propeller wake lengthened and they moved swiftly toward the
island. Grandpa pointed the bow at a narrow isthmus of sand that

split the island into two uneven portions. The smaller portion, to their left, seemed little more than a forested knoll. The right two-thirds was higher, protected from the northwestern winds by a bow of quartz-laced granite that towered above the broad expanse of Namakan lake, reminding the old man of a mossy ship ramming its stone hull against the waves.

"Does it have a name?" the boy inquired as they drew near.

"Blind Pig Island."

"Grandpa!"

"What?"

"You're not fooling me."

The old man thought maybe he did fool the boy too much. Joke, tease, tickle. At times he'd tell stories so fanciful even a child wasn't fooled by them. "No fooling. It's on the Voyageurs National Park map, even the regular map. Blind Pig Island."

Their bow creased the sand. The motor noise died, except for an electric hum as the propeller cleared the cool water. It grew quiet and they listened to the lapping waves and invisible breezes rushing like creek water high in the red pine needles. A breeze with a sharp Canadian chill.

The boy leapt ashore with the rope and tied it to a stunted tree root before turning back to the old man. "Do you need help Grandpa?"

"Do I look like I need help? Just get out of my way."

Dustin was ten that summer. He grew quiet when Grandpa got crabby. That's what Mom told him. Take care of Grandpa, she'd said, but when he gets crabby or talks like he's mad at you, be quiet and wait a minute, he'll get over it. Mom was right. She knew since she was his kid. Grandpa didn't like getting old, Dusty guessed. Too late now, he thought, but the gruffness scared him sometimes.

A cooling swim and roasted hot dogs for lunch. Almost good as fishing. Grandpa held his face underwater, washing his eye. He was an accomplished swimmer and Dusty felt safe in the water with him. They'd brought their snorkeling gear and sometimes people from the houseboats and cabin cruisers lost things overboard. Two summers past Grandpa found a wad of twenty dollar bills floating along below. The old man had kicked his feet into the air and swam down to the money. More than two hundred dollars and Grandpa explained the custom of the sea to him - if it was in the water it was yours.

They unloaded the green cooler of food and drink. Grandpa's beer and his orange soda. The wieners. Ten to a package and he hoped Grandpa would only eat two.

"Can we build a fire right now?" he asked.

Grandpa, tall and large-bellied, stood on the sand arching his back and sticking his fist into it. "Go up there," the old man gestured with his head. "See that little clear area by all the rocks? Seems I remember a fire ring there. Better get going on it if you think you're going to roast wieners. We've been dodging those thunderheads all morning."

The boy squinted across the isthmus to the northwest. Dark, heavy mountains of cloud rose from the far end of the lake, towering into the summer sky, white tops swelling against the blue. Below, in their dark bellies, flashes of lightening brought them to life, storybook dragons born in a treacherous sky. Thunderhead was a fine name Dusty thought, but he heard no thunder. Far below, he saw the lake swept by side curtains of heavy rain.

It was hot and horse flies pestered them, so after they'd gathered sticks and large pieces of birch for a fire, they decided to snorkel, cool off, dodge the flies. Dusty thought it a good plan. Later, he'd cast from the isthmus. Hook a big northern. He was a lucky fisherman. Dad taught him to cast when he was three and he fished all day in heat or rain or wind without complaint.

The chilly water pricked his skin at first, but after a few minutes lost its bite and flowed across his back as if he wore the slick hide of a muskrat. He tasted the rubber mouthpiece. Minnows and small perch darted among the rocks. Fish were strange creatures. They lived in water and died in air. The best thing would be if you could talk to them and they would tell you what it was like.

Blind Pig Island's bulging rock heights sheltered their cove on both sides and the waves were gentle and small. He lost track of time. The water seemed warm now, its chop lessened. Subtle colors slid beneath him - green grasses, brown sand, gray and dark blue rocks. He drifted and kicked and followed a small bass as it dodged among the stones and grasses. Suddenly the water trembled. Thunder cracked and it began to rain in sheets. Hard drops punched the lake's surface, denting it, bringing it to a frothy boil. The distant storm had snuck up on him, thumping from sky to water, and he felt its power against his chest.

He looked up for Grandpa. The island was near but obscured by the downpour and for a moment he couldn't find the old man and his heart skipped. He spit the snorkel and gasped a breath of heavy, rain-laden air. "Grandpa!" he shouted.

The old man, floating weightless on the other side of the cove, felt the raindrops bounding his bare back and dove below the liquid ceiling to escape them. He rolled onto his back and stared up in wonder at this soundless collision of waters, each raindrop dimpling the surface in a tiny splash of silent union. Swimming in lazy circles, he surfaced.

"Grandpa!"

The boy's voice cut the rain and he lifted his head to find him. "Dusty!" he called.

"Here."

"Head for shore. There's lightening."

They arrived at the shallows near the boat almost together. Rain slashed the leaves and needles. Rivers washed down the high clay of the isthmus and made slick mud of it. They tossed their snorkeling gear into the boat and waded ashore.

"I'm cold," Dusty said.

"All our stuff is wet," the old man answered. "Make for the little stand of new balsam there," he pointed. "Won't be dry but better than standing around in a downpour waiting for a lightening strike."

Dusty climbed the bank to the balsam stand and Grandpa jogged back to the boat and retrieved the boy's soaked sweat shirt. "Here." He handed Dusty one end and together they wrung it dry as they could. "Keep your body heat in anyway."

Thunder cracked, rolling across the lake at them. It echoed among the islands and rock promontories, setting teeth on edge. An ominous thrill, keeping them quiet and watchful.

As quickly as it began, it ended.

Minutes later the sky cleared and warm summer sunshine returned. The lake was blue again and the backside of the thunderstorm appeared benign as it rolled off to the southeast.

Grandpa stepped out from under the shelter of the trees. "Come on. Let's see if there's a dry stick left on this island."

All the wood they'd gathered was soaked. For half an hour they scavenged the thick brush, rock crevices and sheltered areas to make their lunch fire. It was hopeless. The downpour had flooded even the most secluded spots they searched. Dusty was discouraged and hungry. "How can we build a fire now?" he complained.

"I can build a fire in a raging blizzard," Grandpa bragged.

"All the wood's wet."

"Not all." He pinched the dead twigs still attached to many of the pine. "Snap 'em. See if they're dry, then rip down enough to get a fire going. Once it's hot we can throw on some bigger stuff and the flames should dry it enough to burn. We don't need much of a fire to roast a few weenies."

Dusty was skeptical of the plan, as he was most of Grandpa's ideas. It seemed that whatever the old man did was slightly more peculiar then what you expected from anyone else. Grandpa was opposed to frowning so Dusty kept a blank face.

Half an hour, and a box of matches later, Grandpa built a fire that was more smoke than flame but did indeed consume the wet wood eventually, leaving behind a hot bed of cherry coals perfect for roasting hot dogs. Dusty ate six. The first three with buns. Grandpa ate two and was drinking beer.

Out on the lake, far to the southeast, a large houseboat labored across the expanse of open water. Dusty watched it almost as he'd watched the minute hand of a clock to see it move. Two smaller fast boats circled the houseboat, then ran off ahead or at right angles. As he watched, one of them veered in their direction though it was still too far away to be sure or hear the motor.

Five minutes later the bow wake was clearly visible and the boat seemed headed directly for the cove. "Grandpa," he said. "Look."

The old man studied the boat awhile. "Chase boat," he said. "Houseboat companies send them out to scout for anchorages. Houseboat's probably towing fishing boats and canoes. Water slide on back, all that. They'll park somewhere for the night so they can play."

"Do you think they'll want to park here?"

"Maybe. Too bad we got here first." He smiled. "Might eat another one of those wieners."

Dusty grinned. "Wanna see my Grandpa belly?" He thrust out his stomach and puffed his cheeks.

They both turned to the noise of the outboard then and the old man noticed the aluminum chase boat was old and deep-hulled. The motor a hundred horsepower or greater. It was running straight for their cove and the operator, who was standing clear of the windshield, had seen their smoke and knew the site was occupied. A chill ran up his spine and he shuddered. Danger coming? Even summer thunderstorms were more predictable then people danger. And harder to guard against. He thought of warning the boy but didn't want to frighten him. The fears of old men, maybe.

The boat operator, a husky young man with short bleached hair, cut the engine abruptly and the chase boat wallowed within hailing distance. "Hey," called the man. "We usually tie up here." He pointed back across the lake at the houseboat. "You about ready to leave?"

It was a commanding voice, Grandpa thought, just short of threatening. He walked down into the water and waded to his knees, closer to the boat. "What's that?"

"I said, this is our spot."

"Got your name on it?"

The chase boat drifted into the cove, swinging sideways to the shoreline. The man put one foot on the gunwale. "Listen here. I've got a houseboat full of people out there looking for someplace to spend the night. Can't just pull in any old place. Two of you in a little fishing boat can go anywhere you like."

"We like it here," Grandpa said.

"I don't want to argue with you about this but national parks are for everybody and we got the greatest need." He shrugged. "I'll give you fifteen, twenty minutes to pick things up here. Takes awhile for a houseboat to move up this far."

As he dropped back behind the wheel Grandpa said, "It is for everybody, and the everybody that's here first is me, so push on somewhere else. We're not moving."

"We'll see about that," the man said. The chase boat roared from the cove and the old man and the boy said nothing until long after the waves from its wake had crashed ashore.

"Is he coming back?" the boy asked.

"Most likely."

"What should we do?"

There was a stone of fear in the old man's stomach. The smart move, take the boy from harm's way, don't let this become a standoff or some kind of test. "Well, I guess we better think of something."

"Shoot 'em." Dusty was angry, and didn't like being bossed by a stranger.

"Crossed my mind." Grandpa led Dusty to one of the large rocks.

"Sit down," he said. "Not a good idea. Shooting."

"You have the gun," the boy said, slipping a little sideways to rest his rump on a smoother spot. "Last year you shot the rabid skunk and you were in the war and you know how to fight. He can't tell us what to do."

The old man stroked his white chin beard. "Punishment don't fit the crime, Boy."

Dusty felt this was a trap. "Okay," he said. "Guess not. Shoot in the air then."

"Shooting leads to more shooting," Grandpa told him. "Anger to more anger. Before long somebody gets hurt, understand?" He stared down hard at the boy. "We don't escalate see? We stay cool, and cool wins. Always does."

"Well, what then?" Dusty was frustrated. "Run away?"

Grandpa's eyes squinted off across the lake where the houseboat labored steadily up the main channel and the chase boats were buzzing around it like horse flies. "We got some time yet," the old man said. "Let's see if we can't figure a way to outsmart 'em."

The boy shrugged. "I'm going to fish over there," he said, pointing to the opposite side of the small isthmus and went to fetch his pole from the boat. If they weren't going to shoot anybody he'd just as well be fishing.

Grandpa let him go, then climbed into the boat and began clanging around in his tackle box. The day was perfect now after the thunderstorm. Golden sunlight sparkled on the water and dried the sand. Wet diamonds flickered in the pine boughs, in the rich green needles.

Dusty flicked his wrist. Heard the high whine of damp line spinning from the reel, sailing in the air, plunking his Daredevil into the water thirty feet from shore. He turned the crank and jigged the rod. Fish would bite now after the storm.

What he wanted was a big northern. They'd keep it in the live well all the way back to the cabin. Grandpa'd cut its head off while it was still alive and fillet it and roll it in butter and flour and fry it hot in bacon fat and eat it so fresh and filled with juice they'd still taste the clean lake in it.

Something struck the Daredevil and Dusty counted to five, on his way to ten, and set the hook. The rod doubled and bowed low over the water. The drag buzzed as the fish ran with the line. "I've got one, Grandpa!"

The old man didn't answer.

"It's big!"

No reply.

Dusty held the fish but only by walking deeper into the lake. He had no net. If he worked the fish into shallow water it might panic, thrash and spit the hook. He wanted Grandpa with a net. "Grandpa!" he shouted again, glancing over his shoulder. No sign of the old man. The boat was empty. The boy was alone.

Grandpa had gone for a swim. The blaze orange tip of his snorkel plowed steadily toward the center of the cove. The old man's idea wanted proving. The situation was simple, he'd decided. One or both of the chase boats would come first. If both came he was afraid no plan would work, but if the first guy was overconfident and arrogant and just mean enough to throw his own weight around, well, then things might be different. Just maybe.

The old man huffed on the snorkel and drew in one quick breath after the next, held the last and threw his knobby legs to the sky, driving his body beneath the surface. He kicked hard, straining his thigh muscles, and reached the bottom fifteen feet below, where he settled into the sand and wavy grass. Around his waist he had fastened a twelve pound weight belt and now he counted the seconds. Two minutes he would need, or a hair less if he was lucky and swift. At seventy seconds his focus narrowed. A demand for oxygen overpowered him, pressing his lungs for release. How many seconds to the surface? Ten? Fifteen? Air expanding as he swam up, relieving the pressure. Yet he held until the ache in his lungs threatened to burst from his mouth. Explode. Drown him. Then up he went, flying against the drag of the weights, until he burst clear, expelled the poison, and drew in sweet fresh air again. His count stopped at 88. Not even a minute and a half. "Shit!" the old man said, pounding a fist against the water. He'd have to try again.

Half a mile away the houseboat came on and the chase boats circled, buzzing closer and closer.

Dusty was close to tears. The graphite rod bent double, its tip circling, dipping the water. His arms and shoulders ached. He feared the fish might drag him deeper and drown him, but even if it did, he refused to quit. The fish was big. Bigger than fish he'd imagined. He dug his heels into the sand and used his leg muscles against the fish, backing once again into waist-deep water.

The fish had not surfaced and was still too far away and too deep for the boy to see his size or if it was even a northern. There were Muskie in these waters and they grew large as barracuda. A walleye can fight too. But a northern usually stayed down, twisting in the weeds and rocks until it freed itself. He understood the fish's panic, the crazy wrestling to twist the barbed hook from its mouth or throat. They were scared the same, he and the fish. And so the boy smiled when the line came clear of the water and he saw wet beads leeching from it, sparkling, slipping away like tiny pearls. Then the pole bowed again, disfigured, bent to the breaking point as he felt the fish circle, struggling to free itself. He saw the muscles ripple in his thin arm as he held it, and in that instant he knew the fish was his. He would take it. Do it alone, without Grandpa or a net. His fish.

Grandpa was on his third skin dive and held his breath for two minutes and two seconds. Just enough time for what he had planned. He glanced at the houseboat when he surfaced. One of its chase boats had broken away and was headed toward the island again. He swam hard for shore.

"Dusty," he called before he had his fins off. "Come here."

He didn't see the boy at first. Across the isthmus he was fighting a fish in deep water. No time for that now. "Dusty. Boy! No time now. Boat's coming."

Still no answer.

Grandpa tossed his fins and trotted across the isthmus. "We only have a few minutes. I need to talk to you."

"Not now, Grandpa. This is my fish."

The old man saw the truth of it in the boy's face. He nodded and went back to the boat for a net. When he returned the boy had backed into shallow water and was gaining line from the fish. The rod was bent like a gaffing hook. Whatever the boy had was big. Hell of a time for it.

He waded into the shallows holding the net high. "See if you can bring him past me, near where I put the net in the water, then I'll take him from behind."

The boy thought it should be his cranking hand, his right hand and arm, that hurt most, but it was his left, his pole arm. It ached from fist to shoulder, like the radiating pain of a well-thrown punch. And he had bit through a fold of skin on his lower lip. He tasted the greasy blood, and didn't remember how it happened. Maybe he'd been grinding his teeth.

He cranked, and saw the fish. A northern. Long. Three feet or more. A thick, rounded belly, yellow-white, deep and wide. His fish was a monster. Rows of teeth and a tail like a great eel.

"Okay!" Grandpa shouted. "Bring him over." The net was in the water.

Dusty cranked, arching his back. The fish pushed itself against the shallow sand bottom and shook its long head. White water splashed and Grandpa lunged. The fish was gone.

They stood in silence. Dusty felt relieved. He'd seen the fish. You didn't release a fish like that. You ate him or you framed him. He was a monster.

"Sorry, boy," Grandpa said.

"It wasn't your fault." The boy reeled in the rest of his line. "I'm okay. Don't even care if nobody believes me. I saw him."

"I saw him too. They'll believe you."

"I hear the boat coming."

"We need to talk."

Grandpa drew him aside and explained what was to come. It was simple enough but the boy wondered if the old man could hold up his end.

"Understand all that?" Grandpa asked.

"Yep."

"See you later," he said, grabbing his mask, fins and snorkel again and wading off among the broken boulders, crowded pines and cracked walls of the cove's south edge. In seconds he disappeared and Dusty stood on the isthmus alone. He walked forward into the water, comforted by the clean feel of it, then stopped there to wait.

He didn't wait long. The boat came on into the cove under full power, only then did the man cut the engine. The sudden power loss caused the wake to overtake the boat and crash against the stern, splashing water over the transom, lifting and shoving the chase boat into the cove. The boy stood firm but it was hard to do. His breath came and went like someone in a race. It was the same man as before.

The boy did what Grandpa had told him. He turned slowly and walked back to shore where he'd left his fishing pole. He picked it up and walked slowly back into the water to face the man, but said nothing to him. Then he made an almost perfect cast out toward the boat and his Daredevil splashed within feet of the wallowing craft.

"Where's the old man?"

Dusty refused to answer, jigging the rod instead and reeling in just fast enough to avoid getting caught up in the bottom rocks or weeds.

"Damn it, boy! I asked you a question."

Slowly, in his head, the boy counted to thirty, but it wasn't easy with his heart pounding against the inside of his ribs like it was.

Each time, Grandpa had said, count to thirty, then talk. He had to do that at least ten times.

"I don't know," he answered finally.

"You're not here alone."

Dusty counted to thirty. "It's a big island."

The man was caught by surprise. He expected trouble from the old man and hadn't counted on facing a boy. "We're bringing a houseboat in here right now," he threatened.

Dusty counted to thirty. It was getting easier and he counted even slower and was taking pride in it. One, he'd say to himself, then two – cast – three. The man frowned. Meanness hadn't worked. He was confused by this.

Underwater, Grandpa swam hugging bottom rocks and grass until he positioned himself beneath the chase boat. He needed air already and it hadn't been thirty seconds. Arching his body he drifted carefully up under the hull and slipped astern.

First, he slid a heavy flat stick between the propeller blades, then with a needle nose pliers he straightened the prop's cotter pin and pulled it. Another thirty seconds and now he was desperate for air and had to talk to himself and calm himself. Time wasn't his enemy. Tension and fear were his enemies. With his left hand he backed out the castle nut, dropped it to the bottom, pulled the prop and dropped it too. Now the worst part, getting back down and swimming to his hide in the rocks. He couldn't surface dive or push off and rock the boat. The only sure way to do it was to expel most of his air underwater, allowing the negative buoyancy of the weight belt to sink him.

It worked. He was on the bottom in seconds. The chase boat disabled. But his vision narrowed and the desperate need to breathe squeezed tears from his eyes. His peripheral vision sparkled with sharp lights like cracks in a sun shield. He swore and prayed and kicked.

It came down to a stroke or two. A few seconds only. Just a few seconds. And in the end his stubbornness won out. He didn't even care if he lost consciousness. This one last effort he made with all his will and what remained of his manliness. Drink the lake if necessary. Die even. But die trying.

He recognized his crack in the rock and swam into it. When his head broke the surface he was crying and trembling. He gobbled a dozen breathes of sweet air before his head cleared and he regained control. He heard the man's voice, threatening the boy.

"Get out of the water. Out of the way. Or I'll move you myself."

Dusty counted to thirty. By now it took him more than a minute and that made him smile. It was the smile that angered the man in the chase boat.

Grandpa slipped unseen from the water and into the pines where he retrieved his towel and clothing. A few minutes later he strolled from the pines toward the isthmus and called out to the man. "Hey! Keep your mouth off that boy or I'm going to have to come out there. Didn't I tell you before that we're staying?"

"And I told you to get out. Houseboat's coming in here."

"Nope," Grandpa said. "It's not."

The chase boat had a four-stroke outboard that hummed in well-mannered authority, just enough so any noise Grandpa had made when he'd been beneath it had gone unheard. The old man smiled. Dusty came to stand alongside him. They'd pulled it off. Dusty smiled too.

"What are you gonna do now?" Grandpa asked the man.

The man was caught off guard again. "Well," he said. "First thing I'm going to do is tow that piece of shit fishing boat of yours out of my way." He pointed. "Then you can swim for it."

"Just bought that boat last year," Grandpa reasoned. "Runs better than that beat up thing you're driving."

Tired of this odd exchange, the man shifted his throttle ahead and the motor roared. The boat seemed stuck and the man increased his throttle, the noise of it echoing from rocks and cliffs. He turned to stare at the motor – a discreet stem of gray exhaust smoke blew parallel with the surface of the water. The boat remained stationary.

"Lost your prop, I bet," Grandpa shouted. "Hot-dogging around no doubt. Guess you can't even move yourself. Who knows where your prop is? Down in the rocks someplace."

The man cut his engine, then pressed the button to raise the motor shank from the water. The outboard was without propeller or castle nut to hold it. "Got a spare?" Grandpa asked.

The man was ignoring him now.

"Can you swim?" Grandpa pestered. "Maybe *you* can just swim for it."

He and Dusty stood in silence as the man ripped open storage compartments and rummaged through them, mumbling. Dusty jerked Grandpa's shorts and the old man bent over. "Where is it?" he asked.

Grandpa grinned. "About fifteen feet right below him," he whispered. "He's drifting though. Should put an anchor out. Lots of these summer boys work up here on the water but can't swim. Come from down south. Met one from Chicago one time. Wore a lifejacket. Ever try to work in a lifejacket? They should stay home where they belong."

The man in the chase boat found his cellular phone on a narrow shelf beneath the steering console. He punched numbers and waited.

Dusty rolled his eyes and told Grandpa, "It doesn't work here."

"I know, but let him play. Eventually he's going to figure out who's in charge now. Keep still and don't spoil the fun."

The man put the phone to his left ear and bent over to talk and slapped his right hand across his other ear. Dusty rolled his eyes. The park didn't have cell towers and the man must've known that since he worked here. "Grandpa," he whispered, "why's he talking?"

"Thinks we're too dumb to know his phone doesn't work. Scare us with the idea of reinforcements. Just watch. This is going to be fun."

The man was speaking into the phone but they couldn't hear anything beyond mumbling. A few moments later he began to gesture as if he were having an animated conversation, and went on in this manner for some time, even groaning once or twice as if getting some bad news.

After he and Dusty grew bored of this, Grandpa called out again. "You can quit pretending now. You're not talking to anybody."

The man ignored him.

"Hey! Did you hear me? Quit playing with that phone."

"Talkin' to me?"

"You're the only one standing in a boat without a propeller talking on a phone without a signal. Yeah. I'm talking to you."

"There's gonna be somebody here in a minute to tow that fishing boat of yours out of here," the man threatened. "I'm putting a houseboat in here."

"Talking about that houseboat out there about a mile that hasn't even turned slightly in this direction? The one with the other boat like yours, but with a propeller? The one that's gone off somewhere else now? That what you talking about?"

The man straightened up, allowed the phone to snap shut, and stared out into the lake. The chase boat must've gone uplake, the houseboat following at a slow, steady pace. In a softer voice, Grandpa said, "You better start thinking about how you're going to get out of here. This fishing boat of mine works. Your phone doesn't work. Your boat can't be fixed. And now it doesn't look like anybody is coming back for you. Maybe they'll never come looking. Might think you're as big a jackass as I do."

Dusty laughed out loud at that one. But then he thought maybe Grandpa shouldn't push his luck since the man was younger and appeared much stronger. It was funny though that he stayed in the boat and made no attempt to come ashore. Maybe he couldn't swim.

Grandpa was in fact thinking along the same lines, and if the guy had a cell phone did he also have a pistol, say, or big knife? No point antagonizing him further. He'd taken the prop from his boat and calling him a jackass wasn't likely to stabilize the situation.

"Listen," Grandpa began in a more reasonable tone. "Can you swim?"

Instead of answering, the man sat back down behind the wheel and sighed. He stared after the laboring houseboat and slowly shook his head. Bested by an old man and a boy. Talk about a bad day, and he'd had a string of them.

Grandpa walked over to Dusty and slung an arm across his shoulders. "Come on boy, how about trying for another one of those northern?" he asked. "I've got a taste for one just now."

"What about him?" Dusty asked.

"Let's give him time to think things over. Get your pole and we'll sort of act natural, then deal with it."

The boy accepted the idea with a lightened heart. He was tired of the tension, and he'd been afraid of the man. He was still afraid but thought now maybe the man wasn't so angry and threatening. Maybe Grandpa was right, if they just went about their business, the man might calm down. Anyway, he wasn't going anywhere, and it sure didn't look like anybody was coming to help him.

The chase boat was drifting a little too, even in the calm water of the cove. Given time it might reach shore, and then the man could step out. But he'd rather fish, so grabbed his pole and trotted back across the isthmus.

Grandpa busied himself rinsing his snorkeling equipment and singing Moon River in a monotone. He wished the man would drop anchor. If the boat drifted onto the rocks and got all busted up that would be more than he'd intended. Sometimes Grandpa knew he didn't consider the long view. Most of his life was spent taking action and he wasn't given to brooding or procrastination. There was always time later to entertain your regrets with a little Irish whiskey and a fine Dominican cigar.

"My name is Gary Kraft," Grandpa addressed the man in a firm voice. "What's yours?"

Puzzled, the man glanced up and answered without interest, "Jason. I work for Summer Sunset Houseboats. SSH. We got fourteen of these boats. If we don't make it in the summer, and summer's barely twelve weeks up here, then we don't make it at all."

Grandpa wandered into the water to his knees again. "Why don't you drop anchor? I'll make a deal with you. Once that houseboat's gone by out there, I'll get my snorkeling stuff and have a look for your prop. Can't be too far away, right? It got you in here."

Jason's mouth curled into a resigned grin. He stood up, shrugged and went to drop anchor. There really wasn't anything else to do, though he didn't expect to see that prop again. Any other day he had a spare onboard, but yesterday he'd given it to a guy, some other old duffer, who'd lost his on a rock. It was always the same out here – amateur boaters unprepared and oblivious. They flagged you down and all but demanded your help. A prop cost two hundred bucks. Did the guy bother to return it? Hell no. Always the same out here.

The anchor caught and swung the boat slightly so its stern faced the smaller portion of the island.

"Do any fishing?" Grandpa asked.

"No time."

"Got time now."

Jason stared at the old man and shook his head. "No fishing tackle."

"Plenty in the boat," he pointed. "You like open face or spin caster?"

"You serious?"

Grandpa walked over and unsnapped two rods from the rubber rack. "You know what they say. 'Every minute you spend fishing adds an hour to the end of your life.' I really think that's true. Taught my son to fish and now my grandson. When you get them past the place where they no longer care if they catch anything, then you've got 'em hooked. Pardon the pun. I mean they learn patience by then."

"I like a surface Rapala in a bay like this," Jason said. "Got one of those?"

"Half a dozen," Grandpa said, and rigged both poles.

The old man swam a side stroke with the poles held above his head. When he reached the stern of the boat he handed them up, flipped his behind onto the swim step, turned and climbed aboard.

"Nice roomy boat," he said.

"Deep hull for hauling," Jason answered.

Grandpa cast west and Jason cast east. They fell into the rhythm. Grandpa had looked the bottom over pretty well and hadn't seen anything that resembled northern habitat in the cove. Dusty was in the right spot for northern.

Line hummed from their reels and lures splashed in calm water. Grandpa thought Jason had pretty good wrist action. The borrowed rod seemed to fit well in his hand and he was patient with the floater, letting it sit awhile before he worked it.

Out on the open lake the houseboat had passed from view. Grandpa cranked and made no mention of it as his Daredevil wobbled not far above a sunken silver propeller catching the filtered sunlight.

Jimmy Olsen

The Private Eye

The guaguita dropped me off on the Tejeda corner. I had on a green shirt that day and it was glued to my back with starch and sweat. Filiberto nodded as I climbed down from the passenger seat and I told Diane and Rebé, who still had twenty minutes to go, that I'd see them at the party later.

"I'm going to dance all night and I'm not going to wear any underwear," Rebé said.

I shrugged. Rebé said things like that.

The guaguita swung left across two lanes of honking, squealing traffic and at the corner went left again. Filiberto. On the street there wasn't a breath of air. I looked up at my windows and saw the curtains fluttering - ocean breezes clearing walled gardens and thick vegetation to cool the apartment. I started upstairs toward the fresh air.

"Hey, there!" I shouted, pushing open the door. It was Friday. I was happy to be home.

"Shhh!" my wife said. "Be quiet and follow me."

Patricia led me to the living room balcony and held me back behind the curtains. "Oh, crap!" she said. "He's gone."

"Who?"

"The private eye."

Patricia never had much of a sense of humor so I knew she wasn't kidding. Life seldom held any irony for her. It was hot in that country and she needed to get a job. "What private eye?" I asked.

"The one down the street in the little green car."

I stepped out onto the balcony and looked up and down Tejeda. Nobody ever parked on Tejeda. "Where?" I said.

"On Calle Two." A cross street. "But he's gone now. Must've seen you get dropped off."

"Well, that's good then. You didn't forget about the party?"

She slid into her rocker and crossed her arms. "You don't believe me."

"Well, I wouldn't say that. Tell me from the beginning."

"Why should I?"

I smiled. "Because I don't think they have private eyes here."

"They're everywhere," she said.

I wanted to change into something cooler but called to the maid, shuffling around in the dining room. "Rosa. Get me a beer, will you?"

"What you want that for?"

"I'm going to drink it."

"You drinking too much, Señor. There's fiesta tonight?"

"Sí, but I'm hot."

"Then take a shower."

"Are you going to get me a goddamn beer or not?"

"Don't you be takin' the Lord's name in vain. I don's hold him guiltless who takes the Lord's name in vain. You hear me?"

"I'm sorry. I just want a beer."

"I get your beer. Ain't no reason to be talkin' all bad."

"I'm sorry. Sorry."

Patricia shook her head. "See how you are?"

"Okay. Tell me why there's a private eye on Calle Two."

"How should I know *why*. He's just there, watching us."

"In a little green car."

"Yes."

"What kind of car?"

"I don't know kinds. A foreign car."

"It's a foreign country," I reminded her. "Most of the cars here are foreign."

"That's not my fault."

"Okay. What does he do?"

"Watches."

"Just looks?"

"Stares up here hour after hour. Watching."

"Ah," I said. "That makes you think he's a private eye?"

"What else?"

"Oh, I don't know. Somebody's chauffeur maybe. Waiting around to pick somebody up."

"Why doesn't he do it then? He's all by himself, and I never see him come and I never see him go."

Rosa carried the bottle of beer in on a small wooden tray. There was no glass but she'd wrapped a napkin around the bottle to give me something to hold. "Your cerveza, Señor."

"Thank you, Miss Pineapple," I said.

"Doan you be talkin' to me any Americanisms." She knocked her worn knuckles against the tray. "You call me Señorita Peña or you call me Rosa, but doan you be callin' me by no norteamericano names. You go on with that, next thing you know a body's soul gets all fonny, doan know what place it supposed to inhabit."

"Did *you* see the private eye?"

"La Doña see him, that's all there's need to be said."

"Okay." I took a long drink and smiled at them. "Well, he's gone now. I doubt he'll be back."

"Oh, he'll be back," Patricia said.

I smiled at them both. It was hot.

Later that evening I backed the Morris onto Tejeda and we started for the party. We'd dressed. Patricia wore a long flowered gown that brushed the tops of her scarlet toenails. I put on the new pink shirt I'd bought in Miami. It had French cuffs and I'd added pink cuff links for accents. We were very colorful.

The sun had set and stars were visible even through the city lights. Rosa had allowed me a couple more beers and I was in a party mood. Traffic was light. We hadn't gone two blocks when Patricia said, "We're being followed."

I glanced in the rear view mirror. "We're in a big city. Of course we're being followed."

Patricia was completely turned in her seat. "The second pair of headlights. Those are the ones. They've been with us since we pulled out."

"We barely just pulled out."

"Is there some reason why you keep calling me a liar?"

A pleasant night, I thought. Starlight. Fresh little breeze. Balmy, in fact. The very kind of a night lovers and tourists yearn for. If only I wasn't a schoolteacher being mysteriously stalked by a private eye. "Listen," I began. "I don't think you're lying. I don't think you're right either. Why would anyone follow us? Me? You? We are not important enough to be followed by anybody."

"Really?" she said.

"Really."

"Why are they doing it then?"

"They're not. You are imagining it."

"I know what I saw."

"And you think he's back there right now?"

"Yes."

"Okay. Let's find out." At the end of the block I spun the wheel and we sped right onto a residential street that led between high

garden walls. I accelerated and we flew down the street two blocks
before I took a sudden left and pulled up to the curb.

Patricia said nothing as we waited in the dark. Minutes ticked by.
A small pickup pulled from a residence gate and turned away down
the street. We waited.

"Are we going to sit here all night?" she finally asked.

"I think we should sit here until we see a private eye. All night, all
day, a week, the rest of our lives. But guess what? There isn't any
damn private eye. Nobody was following us. Nobody ever would."

"Just start the car."

"No."

"You're acting silly."

"Oh, am I? Maybe I'm showing you something. Maybe we're
sitting here so you can see there's nobody following us."

She had a cream-colored macramé wrap with fringes. She pulled it
up around her shoulders. "I feel a draught," she said.

"We're in the damn tropics. There's no stinking draught."

"Oh, I know. No draught. No private detectives. It's just paradise.
Can we go now?"

"Is anyone following us? Yes or no?"

"No."

"Good. Then we can go."

She remained quiet during the rest of the ride. The party was
held above a flower shop where the owner had built a very nice
apartment, then decided to rent it out. The new junior high math
teacher and his uppity wife, who that evening wore a stunning
white dress that clung to every curve, rented the place for what was
a song in those days. There was a night club across the street and
quite a lot of traffic. Not a residential area, which accounted for the
low rent, but the apartment had an acre of balcony space that Mrs.
Math Teacher had turned into a flower garden to rival anything in
the Capital. They were just the kind of people who are successful
at everything without trying, and in the middle of their coffee table

was a fondue pot with a little blue flame under it.

"Good evening," she welcomed us. Her flaxen hair was up. I don't think she was wearing any underwear either. "I'm Eve."

"Adam," I said, leering at her bust.

Her eyes swept me off and came to rest on Patricia. "What a lovely dress." She gripped Patricia's hand. "I'm so glad we've finally met. You don't even know John. Come with me." Patricia was led away.

Most teacher parties were pretty basic – lots of alcohol, cheap snacks and a loud stereo. The music here was maybe Cuban, and quiet. So quiet the nearby night club overpowered it. Nevertheless, it worked somehow. We had our own separate piece of the night into which we sank while quite aware of coarser surroundings. I felt an immediate attachment to the place, the scene, even the host and hostess. I envied the Boswells, in fact. They made me aware of their social superiority. They didn't hold a party, they created one, and the mood was rich, full as the balmy night. I knew others felt it too. We were all instantly inferior to them.

"My wife thinks she's being followed by a private eye," I told the first person I met with a drink in her hand. Her name was Dorka.

She was short and she had dark eyes, dark hair, dark skin. "What's your name?" she asked.

"Clive. I'm the English teacher."

"Where do you teach *the* English?"

"Funny," I said. "We all teach. This is a teacher's party."

"I'm not a teacher."

"Good," I said. "We need some new blood. What do you do?"

"Nothing." She sipped her martini. "I live with my mother."

"Oh. What does she do?"

"Nothing. Lives with me."

"Well," I confessed, "you're the most interesting person I've met at this party."

"Didn't you just arrive?"

"Yeah, and so far it's pretty stimulating."

"We're rich, you see," Dorka said. "And bored." She stepped very close and without touching me with her hands, leaned her soft breasts against my stomach. "You don't have a drink. What can I get you?"

"Beer."

"I think not." She pecked my lips. "I'll be right back, Clive."

I watched her walk away toward the bar, which was staffed by a white-coated man who looked like a rental. Behind me Patricia said, "Who was that?"

"Just some old maid who lives with her mother," I said, turning to smile at her.

"Didn't look like an old maid. She kissed you."

"They do that."

"Are you going to dance with me?"

"After while. I'm waiting for my drink."

"Old maid getting it?"

"Keeps her occupied."

She pivoted and started across the room. "I'll find somebody else."

Other people who were not teachers were arriving. I studied them. No one over forty, and all appeared to have money. The Boswells hadn't been here a year and yet they knew wealthy young people. I'd been here half a decade. I didn't know anybody.

When Dorka returned she had two cigarettes sticking from her mouth. "Take one," she mumbled. "Here's your drink too."

"Scotch?" I sipped.

"Bourbon."

"I don't drink bourbon."

"Well, you are tonight aren't you?"

"I don't smoke either."

"You have to smoke at parties." She took my hand and led me further out near a wrought iron railing. "What did you say about a private eye?"

The remark was a good ice breaker, not a topic. "Nothing," I said. "My wife just thinks she's being followed. More accurately, watched."

She stared across the room. "The one with the flowered dress?"

"Yes."

"Well, she's worth watching. Congratulations. I guess you haven't spent all your time reading Chekhov."

"I'm more of an American Lit guy."

"Oh."

"Don't say 'oh' like that. I guess you're not American."

She smiled. "I'm not, of course, but my problem with your literature isn't that it's written by Americans but that it's so American in its writing. Faulkner, Steinbeck, Stegner. They barely see beyond their own back yards."

"I might argue what they saw close up, was in fact, universal." I thought it was a good line.

She acknowledged it with a tip of her glass. "I do like the boy from Minnesota – Fitzgerald. And Hemingway, of course. He was the great American explorer, claiming a good share of the world for himself, including the Caribbean."

"Where are you from?"

She dropped her half-smoked cigarette into the rich potting soil of a Boston fern and said, "I'm curious about the private eye. Tell me about him."

"Nothing to tell. She imagines some guy is watching our place."

"Imagines?"

"I haven't seen anybody."

"And you don't take her word for it?"

"It's not that."

"What then?"

"Why do women always stick together?"

"We don't. If we did you'd be our lackeys."

"We are."

"Enough. The private eye."

"There's nothing to tell," I said. "I haven't seen anything."

She sipped her drink. "Do you carry a wallet?" she asked.

"Why?"

"Let me see it."

I took it out and handed it over. She set her drink on the railing and opened to my ID. "Hmmm," she hummed, examining the photographs in some detail. "Your mother and father?" she inquired at one point, holding the photo of my mother and father.

"Yes."

"There are people in the CIA here," she said.

"Where?"

She handed the wallet back. "Not inside there. Here. Inside this country."

"So what?"

"Maybe you're in the CIA."

"Did you find a membership card or the lavatory key?"

"Can't be too careful," she said.

"I'm an English teacher. We're not the type to be asked to join the CIA." I tossed the cigarette, which I'd only held and not smoked. "How'd we get talking about spies in the first place?"

"You brought it up. Private eyes."

"Let's settle this," I said. "There's no private eye. I'm not in the CIA. Who are you, really?"

She retrieved her drink from the railing and downed half in one swallow. "Mmm," she said. "If someone's watching your house and your wife saw them, why think it's a private detective? I mean, why not assume a husband watching for a cheating wife or somebody's chauffeur, even a guy looking for a quiet place to sit and think? Is your wife highly imaginative?"

"She's barely imaginative at all," I replied, not intentionally unkind. "I thought of the chauffeur too."

"So her imagination wouldn't run away with her?"

"Never."

She swigged the remainder of her martini. "Then shouldn't you believe her?"

"Private eyes don't follow English teachers, or their wives."

"Well," she said. "There *is* the CIA angle."

"There's no CIA angle."

"So you say. Spies are trained liars."

"May I get you another drink?" I asked.

"I'll do it," she said. "Finish yours off."

"I've barely started on it."

"It's a party. You're supposed to drink the first couple quick and get happy. Sociable. Slow down later so you don't get soused."

I took a swallow and studied her above the glass. "Soused," I said suspiciously. "Not a word common in the speech of individuals who have English as their second language."

"Oh? Is that what English teachers think?"

"That's what this one thinks."

"Drink. Drink," she said, reaching for the glass.

I slurped what I could. Bourbon, like all whiskey, struck me as sweet and sticky. I handed her the glass and she turned toward the bar. A small package, I thought, but well put together. I needed to ditch her as soon as possible.

The large balcony and the two rooms connected to it, a spacious living room and large dining area, had filled while we'd talked. Several people had pulled chairs up to the railing and were resting their feet on the wrought iron grillwork. In the direction of the ocean, I noticed a sliver of moon through the leaves of a large mango. The air was fragrant and filled with laughter from the club across the street. The voices around me were earnest and interesting and when I concentrated I picked out snatches of Spanish and French mixed in with the predominate English of the teachers.

The crowd was large and thick enough for me to disappear. Let

Dorka give my drink to her next victim. If I hung around we might be amusing ourselves at my expense. I crossed over to the farthest railing where a wide-eyed couple were pondering a view of the traffic.

"Evening," I said.

They turned to face me and both smiled brightly. "We're the Tingblads," the woman said. She had dead brown hair and a light blonde mustache. "He's Donald. I'm Signey. We're from Arkansas but we don't talk Southern because we've lived all over the world."

"I'm Donald," Donald said, and we shook hands.

"I'm Clive, the English teacher. My wife is being followed by a private eye."

"You meet such interesting people at parties," Signey said. "We go to parties all the time."

"We love parties," Donald said. He wore a sport coat the color of chick peas. His maroon pants were three inches above the tops of white loafers. No socks.

"It's a teacher's party," I said.

"We're not teachers," Signey told me.

"Oh?"

"Donald's here to write a book."

"Really? That's sort of up my alley. Fiction or nonfiction?"

Donald laughed. "Nonfiction. I've never read fiction. Nobody in my family reads fiction."

"The University of Arkansas gave Donald a twenty-five thousand dollar grant for one year to write this book," Signey said. "He was chosen above all the other candidates. There was almost one hundred."

"Quite a project," I said. "What kind of a page count do you imagine? What's the subject?"

"I'm going to explain this culture to the Arkansas reader," Donald said. "It broadens people's minds to be exposed to other cultures different from their own. With pictures, which I'm taking myself, when I remember to bring the camera," he rolled his eyes knowingly at Signey, "it could end up thirty pages. Even thirty-two."

I stared into the night sky. Pale stars visible above city lights. "My wife thinks she's being followed by a private eye," I told them.

They left me standing there. These were the kind of people who embittered me against my fellow man. I was making less than nine thousand a year and I had five preps. Even worse, I spotted the top of Dorka's head moving through the crowd, searching.

I slipped further into the press of bodies, bourbon on my breath, wiggling among a throng of laughter, pausing behind a large fellow drinking Presidente from a quart bottle.

"Hey," he said.

"Hey."

"Got a light?" he asked.

"Don't smoke."

"Who gives a shit? I just want a light."

"I don't carry any matches either. This is a teacher's party. I'm an English teacher."

"Trying to get some English into these foreigners, that it?"

"No. Literature."

"Literature?" He patted my arm lightly. "Literature. Oh, so sweet. Literature. Sounds a little light in the loafers to me. Know what I mean?"

His face seemed older than his years. A big-headed man. "Listen," I said. "My wife thinks she's being followed by a private eye."

He laughed. "I *am* a private eye."

"Really?"

"After I lost my casino privileges to deal in Reno, all of Nevada actually, I applied for my private detective's license. I got back in the casinos though because I'm the runner up for the Nevada arm wrestling championship. I'm the guy who almost beat Gary Vanpelt. He's got wrists like I-beams."

"What do wrists have to do with arm wrestling?"

"You don't know much about arm wrestling, do you?"

"I know it takes upper body strength," I said. "It isn't the wrists, or the loafers."

He walked to the nearest table and beckoned me. "Sit."

We assumed the position. His hands were massive. His wrists thick.

"Ready?" he asked.

"Go," I said.

He didn't press against me, just held my hand upright and slowly, smiling, he twisted his wrist and laid my forearm gently back onto the table.

"I didn't know there was a trick to it," I said. "You're not the one following my wife, are you?"

"I'm out of the business."

"See you around," I said.

The balcony wrapped away into the dark, hanging over the main street, then around to a side street, ending above a vacant lot filled with trash and several scraggly palms. Lights had been kept low here to discourage guests from viewing a seedy backyard. Some potted greenery was moved there to make dance room in the well-lighted areas. A small table remained, containing a chess set and a flickering candle. I sat down there to hide from Dorka.

"Who you hiding from?" a man's voice asked from the foliage.

"I'm not hiding," I said. "I'm resting."

A tall, thin, redheaded fellow with thick lips slipped from concealment and sat opposite me. He was hot-boxing a cigarette. "I have eight beers left in four ice buckets back there," he said. "Like beer?"

"Yes."

He retrieved two and opened them with an opener hung on a dirty string around his neck. "Do you know who I am?"

"No."

"I'm Wesley MacAfee."

"Oh."

"Never heard of me?"

"Sorry."

"Don't be. I keep a low profile."

"So," I said. "You hide in the potted plants at every party?"

Nodding, he looked left, then right. "I'm talking permanent hiding. Vanished, man. Like gone forever. Smoke. Catch my drift?"

"Not really."

He lit a fresh cigarette with the old one. "I disappeared twenty-two years ago." He smiled, nodding.

"My wife thinks she's being followed by a private eye," I said.

"She probably is."

"Do you know my wife?"

"No. But there are things going on we know nothing about."

"Do you know Dorka?"

"Is that an agency?"

"Agency?"

"Of the government."

"Whose government?"

"Never mind," he said.

I took a long drink of the beer. "Tell me about your disappearance," I said.

"You have no government ties?"

"None," I said. "I'm an English teacher."

"Oh," he said. "I met another teacher here when I first walked in."

"It's a teacher's party."

"Most of the people here aren't teachers."

"I know. About disappearing?"

"I'm in charge of the entire Caribbean geodetic survey." He raised his eyebrows and looked left and right again. "How does that strike you?"

"What does that mean?"

"What?"

"Geodetic."

"I thought you were a teacher?"

"I'm an English teacher. Geodetic sounds like science. I'm not scientific at all."

"Well, it's English," he said. "You should know it. Just means mapping. I'm in charge of mapping everything."

"Everything?"

"Pretty much. We do it all from outer space, of course. Our main office is in DC."

"Of course," I said. "It's taken how long?"

"About a week."

"So where have you been hiding for twenty-two years?"

"Panama first," he said. "Did eighteen years there. Four here now. The trick is to order things. You know, big things. Cars, trucks, forty-man tents. I order a lot of flashlights too. The government likes it if you order a lot of flashlights. Isn't that funny?"

"Nothing surprises me tonight." The beer tasted good and the music was a perfect mix between disco and Cuban drums. "So if it only took you a week to complete the maps of the entire Caribbean, how come the government doesn't send you somewhere else or bring you home?"

"Because they're the government," he said. "Don't you see? That's the beauty of it. I've got a really nice office downtown in the colonial section and a lovely secretary to go with it. I'm a line item on the budget. I haven't been to Washington in twenty-two years, or been visited, or transferred, except for that once, and in a few years I'll retire on a generous pension. I had a lot of friends in Panama. I don't know if it's better here or there. The weather is better here, I think."

"Doesn't the government know what you're doing?"

"Sure. I send them reports all the time."

"Do they think it takes twenty-two years for a satellite to pass over the Caribbean and snap a few pictures?"

He smiled. "You're catching on. The challenge is never to have them ask that question, you see. Bureaucrats change with the years and eventually you become an institution. I'm an entity unto myself with employees, vehicles, facilities and assets. I have a chauffeur and I requisition a new car every other year. They're always olive green. Did you know that was the color of the Geodetic Survey?"

"No. I should've paid more attention in school."

"Do you want to play chess?"

"Can't," I confessed. "In the Navy I was stationed with the runner-up of the Southern California Chess Masters. He taught me everything he knew. I'd probably beat you in four moves or less."

"Who you trying to kid?"

Another sucker. "Suit yourself," I said.

We played for nearly two hours. I beat him, but it wasn't easy. We drank all the beer and got more. "You are good," he admitted. "What were you saying about your wife being followed by a private eye?"

"That was hours ago and I didn't say she was, I said she thought she was."

"Same thing. Why are they following her?"

"It isn't 'they' it's one guy in a little green car."

He smoked. "Hmm. Figures," he said.

"What?"

"I knew you weren't an English teacher. Didn't know Geodetic and you have the logical mind of the analytic personality." Glowing ash reached his fingers. "You're in the CIA."

I laughed. "You sound like Dorka."

"So everybody knows."

"I'm not in the CIA."

"Why's your wife being followed then?"

"Let's just drink."

Patricia found me slouched there across from Wesley MacAfee

who studied me even after he was introduced to her. "So, what do you do?" my wife asked him.

"I'm a drunkard," he answered soberly. "You're the lady being followed by the private eye in the little green car?"

"Yes. How did you know?"

"This man."

"He doesn't believe me."

He nodded, smoking. "That's because it's him they're after."

"I never thought of that," she said smiling. "Come along, Clive. We're going home."

"Already?"

We thanked the host and hostess and said goodbye. They looked exactly as they had when we came in. The rest of the teachers were drunk.

"Do you want me to drive?" Patricia asked in the car.

"Why would I want you to drive?"

"Because you've been drinking heavily."

"I had part of a whiskey, and beer. That's not drinking heavily."

"What happened to Dorka?"

"I ditched her."

"Who was she?"

"Some spy."

"You're so imaginative."

After trying two other gears, I shifted into first and we glided away in the wrong direction.

At promptly eleven-fifteen the following morning, I awoke. Patricia, who needed to brush her teeth, was leaning on my left arm. "Come on! Come on! He's here. He's out there right now. Get up!"

It was the private eye, of course. I struggled from under the tangled sheet. The fan was whirring on high. We had no air conditioning. In the early morning our room smelled fresh, but this late it was muggy, stale, breathless. I was naked except for my shorts.

"Out here!" Patricia urged. She was hiding behind the curtains in the living room again, peering out onto Calle Two. "There he is! There he is!"

I lumbered in and she crouched so I could see clearly above her head. Sure enough, a little green car with some guy sitting in it. "Great. I'm going back to bed."

"Are you crazy? Didn't you see him?"

"Yep. I admit you were right. There's a guy in a little green car on Calle Two. I stand corrected. I'm going back to bed."

"Like hell!" She was angry now. "Do something, and I mean it!"

"I'm going back to bed, or I'm going down and beat the snot out of him, whoever he is. Which is it going to be?"

"You are not going back to bed."

"Okay," I said, and left the apartment without dressing. I have no idea what the little man thought as he watched me jog across Calle Two, but I enjoyed the look on his face. When I got alongside his car he panicked and rolled up his window but neglected to lock the door. I beat on the side of it and kicked with my bare foot. He fumbled with the ignition and started the engine before I had the presence of mind to jerk open the door and haul him out by his shirt.

He kicked and swore. I dragged him almost to the sidewalk before kneeling on his chest. He was quite a small man and my extra weight must've finally convinced him to give up the struggle. He looked at me then and I said, "What in the hell are you doing watching my house?"

I said this in English and he answered in the same language. "It isn't me. It isn't me."

"What are you talking about? I caught you."

"Caught me?"

"Watching my house, you idiot!"

"I'm not watching. I'm eating."

He did have mustard on his shirt. "Why would anybody eat here?" I asked, glaring down at him.

"I work at the customs," he said, pointing toward the ugly five-story government building several blocks away. "I make copies."

"Copies?"

"Copies of copies. Importation documents. We have lots of copies. I eat lunch and take breaks in my car to get out of the building. I can't afford restaurants."

"Oh," I said. "You're not a private eye then?"

"I work for the government."

"You work for the government?"

"Yes."

I helped him to his feet. "Well," I said. "Just don't let it happen again."

"What?"

"Lunch. Don't eat lunch here. You're scaring my wife."

"I like the shade here." He pointed to a large boulevard tree overhead.

"Find another tree. Do you want me to beat you up?"

He got back into his car, roared the engine, rolled down the window and shouted as he drove off, "Gringo!"

When I got back to the apartment I told Patricia it was just a guy who hated Americans. Not a private eye. She seemed disappointed. Then I hollered at Rosa to make café con leche.

We lived there five more years but that was the only time we were watched by a private eye, far as I know.

Jimmy Olsen

Wormwood

That year we lived upstairs in the house of an elderly doctor and his wife on Avenida Independencia. It was on a corner, Independencia and Calle Del Mar, two blocks from the ocean. Across Independencia was an elementary school and playground surrounded by a high dirty concrete wall and across the other way a home where the people kept a large hog, some chickens, and two goats they finally ate.

The doctor and his wife were small, him especially, and they owned a small car for which they had a chauffeur named Julio. There was a maid too, Luz, which is light in Spanish. I don't remember the first name of either the doctor or his wife, but the last name was Abranté. They'd always rented to North Americans they said, and spoke some English, though I don't think they liked Americans much.

Patricia was pregnant about six months with Melanie then, and extremely uncomfortable in the heat. There was no air conditioning but we caught an ocean breeze in the daytime and a cooler breeze from the forested mountains at night. The fresh air and two balconies, one leading off the parlor and another a step down from the kitchen, widened the small apartment quite a lot and we felt very much the adventurous expatriates with so many balconies, and later when the baby was born, Patricia rocked her in an iron rocker on the parlor balcony and watched the hog overturn the neighbors garbage drum.

Late one afternoon we were rocking there, just the two of us, and she said sharply, "Do you have any interest in what happened here today?"

"Sorry," I said. "Didn't mean to talk so long."

"We've been getting robbed."

"Robbed?"

"Burgled."

"Rosa?" I said, immediately suspecting the young girl we'd hired.

"You'll never believe it," she said, shaking her head so her brown hair slapped her cheeks. "Sneaks up the back stairs to the kitchen balcony, sees if the coast is clear and makes her move."

"Who sneaks up?"

"Mrs. Abranté."

"The daring old bitch," I said. "What does she steal?"

"Used coffee grounds."

A tall woman in plastic sandals passed in the street below balancing a laundry basket on her head. Her simple dress was stretched tight across a swollen belly. "Why would anyone do that?" I asked.

"I snuck down the stairs after her and watched through the window. Her and Luz made coffee. Dr. Abranté was called in from his little office and he drank the coffee too. Coffee from our stolen grounds. Have you ever heard anything so demented in your life?"

"No," I said.

"They won't let me use their phone. Mrs. Abranté laughed at me. She's so superior. We can't use her telephone but she thinks nothing of stealing our coffee grounds."

During the day the cotton curtains stood almost straight out from the windows but early in the evenings the breeze grew listless, allowing the supper cooking smells and goat dung to mix with whatever had washed ashore. "If there's an emergency," I said, "we'll just go down there and use the phone. We don't need permission in an emergency."

"If I wasn't so pregnant and fat and tired, I'd find a job."

"You know there's no jobs." Across the rooftops toward the sea, it seemed like the sun rested on the Hispañola Hotel. "Not for a gringa, anyway."

"Guess what else," she said pouring two fresh rums. "They're all laughing at your legs because you keep wearing shorts after I've told you *how many times* men here don't wear short pants."

"You saw them laughing?"

"Luz told Julio and he likes Rosa so he told her and she told me." She placed her drink on the balcony ledge and gazed past me toward the green hills. "They call you Patas de Gallina. Chicken legs."

"Suppose they think it's funny."

"I do."

The hog house across Calle Del Mar was square and boxy and flat-roofed, made of concrete like ours, but ours was all rounded corners and tall. The house across reminded me of a rooftop pigeon cage where different birds fly in and out and you watch but can't distinguish one from another. The same was true of the people who lived there, and we discussed the look-alike people quite a lot.

I wanted to discuss them now instead of talking about my legs. "Who's that guy?" I pointed. "Have we seen him before?"

Patricia liked talking about them too, she was a great people watcher. "Sure," she said. "He's the husband or boyfriend of the old lady's fat daughter. Not the short fat one but the fat one with long hair."

"I don't think so."

"I'm telling you. That's who he is."

"No. I think he's a new one and we've never seen him before."

"You've been seeing new ones every day since they got robbed."

"Not every day."

"Almost."

We'd watched a robber - we thought he lived there - walk in one afternoon and take cash from two of the bedrooms and help himself to a plate of chicharron de pollo from the dining table and walk out and down the street munching away. Some of the people inside finally chased him and we watched that too. We didn't catch on and it got around that the norteamericanos just sat on their balcony drinking rums while their neighbors were being robbed. What can you expect of foreigners?

"I don't think we should do anything about the coffee grounds," I said. "You'd just throw them out anyway."

"I didn't say we should *do* anything. I just told you about it."

"Dr. Abrante' said last week that Julio would drive me to a used car lot on Saturday and he'd come along to translate. We've got to get a car."

All that happened before Christmas and other things happened too, which I forgot. I bought the car that Saturday for one thousand, six hundred pesos; a lot of money for a ten-year-old car in those days. But hardly anybody there had cars then.

It was the only foreign car I ever owned. A British Morris, gray and shaped like a Volkswagen Beetle but with the engine where it should be and a trunk with a hump. In the floor of the backseat there was a hole big enough to stick both feet through. No door on the glove compartment and it got forty miles to the gallon. James A. Michener rode in that car once and didn't say much, but that was a year later before Patricia had her accident and wrecked it.

The new year didn't start out very well for us and the Abranté's. It was because of a book. I went down to beg a phone call. Standing in their darkened parlor heavy with black furniture, I shifted from one foot to another to avoid the clouds of tiny mosquitoes hovering

under the tables, chairs and lamp stands. They refused to install
screens. Upstairs we burned green coils that gave off a toxic yellow
smoke and left a gray ash. Mrs. Abranté led me to the phone and
saw I was carrying a copy of a novel I was using in class then, *The
Ugly American*. She called the doctor in and he read the title and
they discussed it in both Spanish and English and then told me how
funny it was that I was an American reading *The Ugly American*.
I never saw the humor in that, and when I didn't, it made it all the
more funny for them. They never got over it and the more they
thought about it I guess, the better it sounded.

They laughed at me unexpectedly sometimes after that. Mrs.
Abranté's saggy black eyes mocked me, flicking along my pale
skin to settle on the perpetual sweat of my forehead. "You sweat,"
she used to say, suggesting that I came from an inferior race that
couldn't hold in its sweat. I was young then, not ugly, but sweat
ugly to her, and if so, maybe to anyone there. White men seldom
entertain thoughts of racial inferiority and I was puzzled by it until I
understood it.

In April when it really got hot again we ate our suppers on the
balcony. Melanie was four months old by then and Patricia doted on
her.

"Now she's telling me I can't play cards with Rosa," Patricia said
between spoonfuls of plaintain and chicken liver soup.

"Mrs. Abranté?"

She nodded, catching the dribbles with her napkin.

"Why can't you?"

"Some kind of no fraternization policy."

This made me laugh. "And all the time her and Luz gossip about
every move we make up here. Talk about fraternization!"

I leaned over to be sure they weren't listening. The house had a
small yard they called a garden and it was L-shaped with the long
part on Independencia hidden behind a wall. The garden had one
tree, a palm, ringed with croton and some kind of vine that climbed

straight up almost to the coconuts. They had some green grass there too. Julio and Mrs. Abranté watered it three or four times a day. Julio cut it twice a week with a machete that had a broken tip.

"Are they listening?" she asked.

"No."

"I don't care what they say. Rosa's the only friend I've got and we like to play casino in the afternoon. She wins every time."

I finished eating and had to wipe the sweat from my face even though the sun had gone completely and it was very dark. The city had poor street lighting but the nights were alive with music and laughter and though it was all foreign to us we'd come to like it because we could hide in the dark of the balcony and watch and listen. We talked softly and I smoked a cigar sometimes.

"She's your maid," I said. "You can play cards with her if you want to."

"She's more like a friend. It's a nice break for us when the baby takes her afternoon nap."

"If you say so I'll take my ugly face and go down there tomorrow and tell them both to quit pestering you about it."

"You'd really do that?"

"Well, I don't want to, since they let me put the car inside the wall." They had an extra iron gate on the Independencia side and let me bring the car in there so it wouldn't be stolen or stripped. Anything left out at night was gone in the morning. We got rid of a laundry basket full of termites that way once. "I'll do it, though," I said.

"Never mind."

"Remember how long we looked for this place? Two months in that hotel without a car. That's what took almost all our money, but that doesn't mean they should pester you about the maid."

"I said never mind."

That was the night before Patricia lost her temper.

I came home around four. The house had an outside stairs straight from the ground to the kitchen balcony, and around front an enclosed granite stairs spiraling up from the main door. That day I entered by the main door and the fight was already in progress out back. Can't say I was too surprised about it. That fight had been coming a long time.

Patricia has a deep voice and when she raises it, it can be heard for some distance. Inside the concrete walls her voice had a fine acoustical quality and reminded me of that Pentecostal preacher who works El Conde in the afternoons.

"This is disgusting, sickening!" she thundered. "You expect us to live like pigs?"

"What do I care how you live?" I recognized Mrs. Abranté's heavily accented voice. She spoke English very precisely because she'd learned it from a book.

"Why won't you come up here and look for yourself? Maybe you'd like to eat off my cupboard. I'll make you a sandwich. Come on! I dare you!"

I entered the kitchen and Rosa was standing near the door, well back, hand clamping her mouth. She did this whenever she laughed to cover the gap where her front teeth were missing. Mrs. Abranté was not in the room and Patricia's broad back was to me and she was shouting at the open balcony door.

"No one likes your food," Mrs. Abranté told her from somewhere below.

"Come and see why then," Patricia said. "Come on up. I dare you! Come on."

"What's the matter?" I asked.

Patricia spun around, surprised to see me. She pounded the kitchen cupboard with her fist. She has big hands and the force of her blow overturned some cups and the salt and pepper shakers. "Look at this," she ordered.

The cupboard was old, worn like everything there. Most of the white paint had peeled, leaving brown wood heavily grained and soggy almost like something waterlogged. "Needs paint," I said.

"Look closer."

She scared me a little the way her eyes darted, unfocused, so I examined the cupboard carefully. It was ripe with narrow white worms - bone white and corpulent, with hard golden heads. "Pretty bad," I said. "Lucky we didn't get sick."

"Not that that old bitch cares! How many maggots do you think got mixed in the baby's formula? How many?" Her face was very red and spittle had collected at the corners of her mouth. "Now! I want it replaced now!"

Mrs. Abranté was gone when I looked down the stairs. "She wouldn't listen?"

"She left?"

"Yes."

"She better not leave."

"She's gone."

She looked for herself and when she came back I thought she seemed more composed. "Fine," she said. "But she forgot to take her maggots with her." There was a small iron pan on the stove and she swung it up against the rotting wood, splintering the corner. Rosa gasped and ran away.

"Honey," I said.

"Help me."

"This won't solve anything."

"Help me!"

Together we battered the wormy wood until it loosened pretty much in one piece. We threw it down the back stairs so it landed hard against Mrs. Abranté's back door. "My baby doesn't eat maggots!" Patricia shouted.

There was no answer.

We moved out of that house in June and I never saw the Abranté's again or heard anything about them.

I never thought much about them either because so many more

memorable things happened there during those years and it wasn't until today, a lifetime and thousands of miles away, for no reason I thought about them. I was tired of trolling and the motor sounded rough so I anchored and slipped my shoes off to see if I could tan the tops of my feet, which seemed to stay white all summer, and the Abranté's popped into my head. They appeared with such clarity I heard their voices and smelled the hot peanut oil Luz used in nearly all their cooking. They must be long dead now, but I remember everything exactly. The memory though, unlike the truth, has lost its bitterness.

Jimmy Olsen

Hurricane *Georges* Journal

At a small apartment hotel in Santo Domingo we awaited the arrival of Hurricane *Georges* and the next home run by local hero Sammy Sosa. *Georges* was reported to be a category five hurricane, feeding on the warm waters of the Eastern Atlantic, thrusting westward toward Puerto Rico and the Dominican Republic. In neighborhood colmados and cafes television sets were tuned to ESPN. Sammy would surely hit 64 or 65 before the lights went out.

The hotel was six years old, built by a German named Don. A concrete monolith, five and one half stories high, painted to a rich peachy pastel, stylish as a tombstone. Unlike older architecture of the Dominican capital, it lacked the high ceilings, generous balcony space and comfortable roominess that characterized the Latino Caribbean.

The hotel's unattractiveness convened at its entrance, a perfect rectangle of concrete, glass, and granite tile - a three-sided bunker, housing a small bar and several tables. To the right, a glass office staffed by an attractive female reservation's clerk. In the event anyone should become disheartened enough to drink there, staring down the noses of automobiles parked within six inches of the entrance, the clerk also bartended. Beyond the cars, the view was that of a narrow and noisy street, four garbage barrels and two concrete utility poles. Across the street stood a high concrete wall behind which lived an exceedingly rich old couple, so I was told by an Italian.

Light rain was falling in late afternoon and we wondered if it was the beginning, or just rain. My son Keith stood beside me as I smoked a very good cigar, "They're at it again," he said, tossing his head up in the direction of our fourth floor suite.

"I know. I saw the door close."

"You can hear their voices but can't make out what they say." He hawked and spit into the rain. One of his habits I disliked. "Think they'll chicken out?"

For almost 24 hours my daughter and her husband had debated. He wanted to call the airport, change the tickets and fly to safety in Miami, or Iowa, where they live. She wanted to stay.

"They've got a baby back home to think about," I explained. Blue smoke curled out and mixed with the rain. "I promised to take them to the airport if they decide to go but I've tried to stay out of it."

"But you and I and Mom are staying, right?"

"We're staying." He wanted to stay because he'd never seen a hurricane. I stayed because I had.

"Do we go down in the basement like a tornado or what?"

I shook my head. "They're going to tape the windows."

"What does that do?"

"Wrecks your view."

He smiled and made a face. "Dah!" Yesterday he shaved his sideburns, leaving a narrow strip of untanned skin on either side of his head.

"I really don't think it does anything but make everyone feel better," I continued. "If the wind is strong enough it'll shove the frames and everything in. Tape can't stop that."

"So what *can* stop it?"

"Nothing."

"Great. We just die then."

"That's one option. Or, we might try staying away from the windows during the storm."

He seemed to tire suddenly of my company, or my pat answers, and turned to go. "I'm going to find out what they're saying," he said. He had a way of throwing his shoulders forward as he walked that made him look hunched and cave-chested.

That was Sunday. The rain let up in the evening and Patricia and I walked to the colmado on the corner where we sat outside on the sidewalk in plastic chairs for several hours drinking. She had rum and coke in a Styrofoam cup and I drank Presidente so cold there was ice stuck to the bottles. Dominicans - noisy, friendly - came and went, lugging purchases of beer, sweet pastries, cigarettes, chilled pigeon eggs served with onions. They included us in their conversations, especially those about Sosa, nodding approval at our choice of him over McGwire.

Patricia leaned close to me and said in English, "It's just as loud and dirty and disorganized as I remember."

I nodded toward the wall-mounted television. "They're bored with the hurricane already. Interrupts *béisbol*."

"Maybe they're just waiting to see what it'll do to Puerto Rico."

"Puerto Rico's 90 miles from the east coast. Too late by then. Satellite photos are pretty frightening. Well-defined eye, thick clouds churning out a couple hundred miles or so. Looks mean as hell. It'll never notice Puerto Rico."

She seemed uncomfortable and frowned. "Why don't we leave then?"

I had no answer. Maybe because we'd waited so long to come back.

The next morning *Georges*, a chopping wall of wind, sliced across

Puerto Rico and slammed into the east coast of Hispañola. Its speed over land slowed from fourteen miles per hour to eight. Its winds one hundred twenty to one hundred forty miles per hour. On the television in the colmado they'd begun to pronounce *Georges* with italics. Sarcasm directed at the French, as if they were somehow to blame.

In Santo Domingo it was a half decent morning. Pale sunshine and high cirrus clouds that didn't look particularly menacing, though people had started mobbing supermarkets and gas stations. We'd done all that two days before, stocking up on rice, beans, five-gallon jugs of fresh water, beer, ice, canned foods, candles and Spam.

"Spam?" the question was posed by Keith.

"Can't have any kind of natural disaster without it," I'd explained. "Just isn't done."

"Even if we all die or get blown into the ocean I'll never eat Spam," he predicted, wrongly, as it turned out.

By noon the clouds had thickened, darkened, lowered. They moved more rapidly with a discernable counter-clockwise flow. Still, I thought them more mesmerizing than menacing, like some trick of time-lapse photography, and I dizzily marked their swirl across the top of the hotel.

Several hours before, Don the German had become a fixture at the entrance, smoking Marlboro Lights and frowning at the sky. He'd ordered plywood cut and nailed to the office windows. Tables and chairs were stacked behind the bar and he kept one maid in constant attendance sweeping leaves from the speckled tile as the wind freshened. The rain was light and intermittent.

I waited until he was alone and unoccupied. "I'm the guy who has his family in 427," I said.

"Of course," he answered, barely glancing my way. We were of similar height, though he was lighter built. His face was thin and rough with a two or three day beard partially hiding a nasty scar on his upper lip. I guessed his age as mid-30s.

"What's the latest?"

"His eye pass La Romana." He spoke heavily accented English. La Romana was a smaller city less than 50 miles away. "What happens when the lights go out?"

He slid two steps to his right and pointed to a large steel grate in the concrete parking lot over which a truck had been parked. "Planta," he said, using the Dominican term for generator or power plant. "Three weeks fuel supply." He spoke confidently and the voice matched the man. "I have a well. Plenty water. We are safe here. He don't hurt you."

I began to fear then that he saw a panicking guest. "This is good," I said in a strong voice. "You seem well-prepared."

"Self-contained," he said rather triumphantly.

"I see that."

"He is bad," the German continued after examining my face closely for any signs of hysteria. "The eye pass directly over us, I think. After he pass, it is the worse then."

I nodded agreement. "When the wind changes."

"Yes." He cocked his head. "You have seen hurricanes before?"

"Several," I said quietly. "You?"

"Of course." Then a moment later. "But never one so big."

"When will you turn on the generator?"

"It is automatically. When the light go out the planta is coming on." He gazed fondly at the steel grating. "In the night she stop for two hours and once in the day to make the oil change and to give her the rest."

"Very sensible," I said.

He smiled briefly at my understanding of machinery. A Dominican, of course, would run the generator day and night until it seized. We both understood this and understood too, that after the storm we would face our most severe test. A city without power or fresh water. Without ice for a cool drink in the tropical heat, five million toilets that didn't flush. Rotting meat and vegetables. The uncooled bodies of the dead.

"Many will die," I mused.

"Many."

"The poor."

"Yes, of course."

Thousands lived in shacks along the Ozama River and many more in denuded gullies on the fringes of the capital. In the hills and mountains, thousands more. The wind would sweep their homes and torrential rains bear the remains to the sea. On the beaches along the Malecón where the tourist hotels stood, they would come to search for the bodies among the litter and swollen corpses of the animals.

"If my wife should come down, tell her I went to the colmado."

He grinned. "The beer is cold awhile longer."

I walked away from the hotel. Clouds streamed above, forcing me to look down or lose my footing. Dominican sidewalks are neglected and perilous, littered, broken and fraught with sudden, deep holes leading to the sewers. I zigzagged.

SuperColmado Maximo Gomez was bustling. I recognized two of the regulars who nearly always faced one of the two television sets on the walls. Victor Torres, the only person behind the counter who spoke English, acknowledged my arrival with a smile and nod. "Presidente bien fría?" he inquired.

"Sí."

The iced green quart bottle was handed across and he dashed away with the limp cash. Unlike the others, I preferred to sit on the narrow sidewalk near the curb where I could see activity inside the store and out, speak to the water delivery man as he came and went on his motorized bicycle, nod at the small groups of uniformed students carrying books, observe the flashy men in their new cars talking on cell phones and pulling to the curb against traffic to demand beer and cigarettes. Merengue drifted from behind a curtained window of a second floor apartment next door, mixing with salsa throbbing from car stereos. People shouted, children darted between the chairs, pedestrians, traffic. Automobile horns bleating without reason, and above all else, much laughter.

The nature of a place is determined by inhabitants more than vicinity, even ambiance. The Hawaiian Islands inhabited by Polynesians is paradise, inhabited by Americans it's a glass and concrete tourist trap. The Dominican Republic inhabited by Dominicans is dirty, musical, disorganized and friendly. The same people who would rob your home in the night might save your child's life the next morning or hand you over their last peso.

Life here taps to the beat of each single heart, raucous, lacking the order of North American society, lacking too the justice, and the fated boredom. Each individual demands center stage and the demand is granted until the noise is deafening. It's why I always loved the place. It can't shut up.

Patricia pulled up a white plastic chair and joined me. "How come you didn't order me something?"

"Didn't know when you were coming."

"Rum and Coke."

I waited on her and when I sat back down said, "I was thinking how I love this place."

"I thought we left because you were tired of it." We'd been gone twenty-five years. "Tired of the blackouts, nothing done on time, nobody to fix your Jeep."

I stared down at a piece of orange peel blackening on the broken concrete. "There was this hot afternoon once around 1974 or 1975 and I was alone driving along the Malecón toward the aduana and I had that moment. I didn't want to be anyplace else or be anybody else. Driving, sweating in the afternoon heat and it was all so perfect. That was the greatest moment of my life."

"How many beers have you had?"

"Maybe it should've been like the game-winning home run, my first bestseller or something, but that's Hollywood. Life is different. Better. Not outside things, inside things. That day, I was driving to the aduana to bribe some guys to get my scuba gear out. The customs broker had already bribed them once but something had gone wrong and he'd about had it he said, and I don't know why but I knew I'd do it, and I did. But it was much more than that, it was knowing there weren't a handful of people on earth doing what I was doing or had dived the places I'd dived and found what I'd found then. I could swim for miles and not get tired and in that truck that day nobody on earth knew where I was and if they did I felt like they'd be so envious they'd croak. A breeze coming off the Caribbean, traffic noise, my arm so tan, proud to be sweating in the tropical sun. Everybody else on earth was selling insurance."

"You know, you've only been sitting here twenty minutes." Her jaw muscles twitched. "Is that why we're back, waiting to get clobbered by a hurricane, so you can recapture some kind of goofy youthful epiphany?"

She didn't understand and I should've known that. "It never happened again," I explained.

"You want to be 26 years old, and you want to sweat?"

"You making fun of me?"

"I'm waking you up. Drink another beer."

"I will." I walked to the bar.

Twenty-five years ago we left Santo Domingo on our annual summer vacation to the States and forgot to come back. Our return now was a pilgrimage, but tragically it isn't the same *you* who returns but an older version, filled with rosy memories and over-ripe expectations. Instead of $7.95 lobster dinners and Old World charm, you find McDonalds and inflation. Hurricane *Georges* appeared as the one bright spot in the firmament.

Victor reached for my empty bottle and said, "You are staying at the aparta hotel?"

"Yes."

"It has a planta?"

"Yes."

He glanced over his shoulder before continuing. "We have a small one but it won't last long after the electricidad is gone. Maybe I will come to visit you. What number is your room?"

"Four twenty seven."

"Norteamericano." He grinned. "You have made much ice?"

"Yes."

"Tomorrow I will bring a bucket."

So there it was again, unchanged since the 70s and long before. Our place in the hemisphere. Iceman. "Keep your mouth shut," I told him. "I don't want people standing in line. You might not get any."

Victor went for my beer. I squinted at ESPN. Baseball, the lifeblood of the nation. I was glad Dominicans had Sammy. His bat seemed to beat back the storm.

When I sat down again Patricia said, "I don't think the kids are going home."

"Good."

Keith came along the broken sidewalk wearing beige corduroy shorts and shower shoes. "Game on?" he asked.

"Guess so," I said.

He nodded, stepped inside and ordered a beer. He was under age. Dominicans don't concern themselves with such constraints to individual freedom. Would, in fact, hand over a beer to any child with the cash. I'd come to favor laissez faire. Let them learn to drink early, instead of mopping their blood up from a country highway on prom night.

Keith got his beer and sat with his back to us, joining the spectators in a row of chairs inside the colmado. The television was mounted to the wall behind the counter. I watched him awhile, a short-haired boy who'd never been to Santo Domingo, spoke not a word of Spanish, acting bored, slumping in his chair. Why did the locals accept him? Include him in their remarks about the game? What's the matter with this place?

Nearly two hours passed before the wind picked up and we headed back to the hotel, clothes flapping against our bodies. The rain held off.

A small crowd of residents gathered at the hotel entrance, standing along the concrete walls, some with cameras, some with bottles. The sight of my rented minivan worried me. I hadn't bought the insurance.

The sky darkened. Street lights flickered. Less than half of them came on.

"Hasn't even started yet and the lights don't work," a man said in Spanish.

The wind shrieked. The last of the lights winked out.

"I'm going back up," my wife told me.

Keith followed and they marched single file up the granite staircase. The German reappeared in a tight Speedo, crush-proof pack of Marlboro Lights visible alongside his privates. His toenails were clipped short and he had rather large feet for a man his size. "You look ready," I told him.

"He won't get me," he said. I smelled rum on his breath.

The wind howled. Palms along the boulevard and in the fenced yard directly across bent at the waist, their fronds gathered and beaten. One by one they lost their coconuts. Their fronds whipped, shredded and blew away. The tiled roof on the house behind the wall began to clatter and clay tiles picked themselves up and sailed high above the city to be lost against a churning sky. The sound of the wind was a scream.

The Caribbean's best weather is between storms at the beginning of the hurricane season, early September. Rates were low, but if your luck ran out it cost you.

"It's going to go!" an onlooker screamed, pointing down the street toward McDonald's.

"What's going to go?" my daughter asked from behind my shoulder.

"Where'd you come from?" I said.

"The rest are stuffing towels in the window tracks and corners. I came down to see how you're doing."

"It's going!"

We leaned out to see the McDonald's "M", the golden arches, atop its steel tower. The thick steel buckled like the cheap plastic it flaunted and toppled soundlessly through a series of power lines and onto the street. A cheer rose around us and we cheered loudest. Destruction of this flag of our national mediocrity yanked from us a spasm of unrehearsed joy. Had we taken time to think it over we might've been offended.

Rain blew from the sky. A sudden deluge overpowered the air.

"It's coming in sheets," my daughter told me.

"See the streets fill up."

The sound of trees ripping. Branches beat against the corner of the building. Leaves littered the street, sidewalk, the parked cars started to jump. The wet German smoked.

The sky was swallowed in water, the streets disappeared. We had to be careful about not sticking our heads out from the shelter of the bunker. All the spectators were soaked and water dropped steadily from the stairs, flowing from the doorway and across our feet. Trees died in thuds and began to fill the streets and yards, ditches and roofs.

The storm strengthened. The wind was a close and mortal thing. Powerful. Palpable. We spoke in bursts. The narcotic speech of senseless spectators. I was ankle-deep in water from the stairs. The upper floors were flooding, I told the German. He climbed.

"Afraid?" I asked my daughter.

"Kind of gives me the shivers."

It was true. We were more awed than frightened.

"I'm going up and check on everybody," she continued.

"Be careful."

"It's just water and wind."

Her oversized T-shirt was soaked and stuck to her. "Come back and tell me what's going on up there," I called to her back. "It'll be dark soon."

The streets were abandoned. Traffic had stopped. Tiles continued to launch from the roof across the street, giving up one by one or peeling off in rows. I wondered about the old people inside. Were they cowering or had they seen it all before?

A público made its way along the street. Its flashers going. Single driver, no passengers. On the back window as it passed we saw a number in duct tape - 64.

"Nuestro héroe Dominicano, Sammy. And the game is not over yet," said the large man to my right.

Three 55-gallon drums rolled along the street, two abreast and one behind. They passed the público on the right and moved off, bouncing against the curbing and over the debris.

I glanced at the large man and asked did he speak English. Yes, he said.

"I don't know how to say spectator in Spanish," I told him.

He chuckled and placed a hand on my shoulder. "Espectador," he instructed. "Similar, no?"

"Yes," I said. "I don't like it though."

He nodded and was quiet awhile. "The difference," he said, "is between watching what you can't change or watching what you should change." He passed me his bottle. "Is this a thing of God or Satan? When it finish, I know it will be left to us to bury the dead."

"Where are you from?"

"Santiago and New York."

"Which is your home?"

Puzzled, he backed against the wall, taking his bottle. "I'm not sure." He drank, held the bottle at arm's length to examine the label. "Brugal or Bermudez? We Dominicanos can argue such questions, but Sosa or McGwire? Never. He is our brother." He tucked the bottle into the waistband of his pants. "So I live in New York but my heart is in Quisqueya. It's often so," he said, and laughed. "Even with women."

Three drunkards came along the street - two men and a woman. They were dragging the golden arches and the woman fell repeatedly, cursing in both Spanish and English, foul oaths that caused her companions to render assistance until she regained her feet and curbed her tongue. As they passed, often losing their collective grip on the plastic when the wind grabbed it, she stopped in the street and stared at us.

Her face was ravaged by drunkenness - dead eyes, slack lips, and entangled mess of wet hair like a witch. "You bastards!" she accosted us. "Look at you! Hiding in a doorway. Afraid of the storm. Afraid of the wind. Afraid of the rain. Impotent bastards!"

"Get that drunken bitch away from here," the big man told her companions. "Why do you follow a puta like that? Sons of whores."

Surprisingly, no one argued with him and all three staggered away up the street. I noticed the golden arches were cracked and wondered where they would hang it. A living room wall? The arches were taller than a man. Their favorite bar maybe or a lawn ornament.

"The looters are even worse," the big man told me, offering the bottle again. "There will be gangs of them already. I will carry my revolver for the next two weeks at least. You should stay inside the hotel. They like to rob foreigners, especially Americans. I don't suppose you have any weapons?"

"No," I said.

He shrugged. "Probably better. The police don't like Americans either."

"Nobody likes us," I complained.

"Do you expect them to?"

"Well, I guess not, but why do they all want to come and live with us then?" It occurred to me too late that I might've been better off keeping my mouth shut.

He only smiled. "You don't understand yourselves. What do you think you are to the world?"

"I'm not a politician."

"It's not politics," he said. "It's envy. People want what you have but they don't want to do what you had to do to get it. Understand?"

"Not really."

This didn't seem to surprise him. "Americans don't look at themselves from outside. It's a big country," he said. "I lived in St. Louis for awhile when I was at the university. People there would ask me stupid questions about my country. *Do we own it? Where is it? What language did we speak?* And it's not that I'm offended by this, just surprised that Americans are so stupid. I'm not trying to offend you, I just mean we can't imagine you as stupid."

"Or poor," I said.

"It's just that America is a great country. It seems greater than the people themselves."

I nodded. "Common complaint."

"I think it is because of arrogance," he said. "You have too much of everything, you earned it, which makes you too proud."

This was the very kind of discussion I'd always avoided when I lived here. Any defense sounded like blatant nationalism, unless I trashed my country, a common strategy heard too often from Americans. "No one lives up to the ideal," I said. "Money makes for arrogance anywhere. True, most Americans don't know hard times, media says stupid things like America's the greatest country, New York's the greatest city. I know it sounds conceited but we don't mean it as an insult. Really."

"Ah, ha!" he said, and moved closer to me. "You want the world to overlook your conceit and accept your ideals, too?"

"Many do I suppose."

"Why should we?"

I smiled. "I thought you had already. Isn't this a democracy?" I sighed. "How many choices are there. Trujillo and the secret police?

Or go the other way and end up like Jamaica?"

"Of course this is a democracy," he said.

"Then why are we arguing?" I smiled diplomatically.

"We are only discussing."

"Good," I said. "I love this country. One of my children was born here."

"¿Verdad?"

"Really. She kept her red passport too."

"¡Muy bien!" he said, passing the bottle.

I held the bottle to my lips with both hands and still the wind seemed to have a stronger grip. I sucked at the rum and handed it back, nodded and found the stairs.

On our floor, my son and son-in-law were pushing water out the door. Others along the hallway were doing the same and everyone seemed in good spirits. Banging from somewhere above, high-pitched whistling of wind loose in the rooms, restricted conversation. When I walked inside I heard the telephone. The Germans owned the telephone company and had managed somehow to keep the phones working. I picked it up and said, "Hello."

"What are you still doing there?" My cousin's daughter at the American Embassy.

"Just got back from having a couple beers."

"Are you crazy? Get over here right now. There's still time." She hung up.

Patricia wrinkled her nose at me and asked, "Who was that for crying out loud?"

"Riña." Our name for her because she was feisty and now after a couple years with the Peace Corps she was a Latin American expert, that seemed now to include the weather as well.

"Still after us to go over there?"

"Thinks we'll be safer huddled with our countrymen."

Patricia smiled. She has a big smile with most of her upper gums in it. "Let's have a party," she said. "Like the old days."

"Who do we invite? We don't know anybody."

"The whole floor, or anybody else who wants to come."

"Okay," I said. "We got plenty. You going to cook?"

"Who else?" She was barefoot and her toes were wrinkled.

"Then I'm in. You make better rice and beans than any Dominican who ever lived."

The boys stopped sweeping to listen. "Knock on some doors," she said. "And find a good radio station."

Our electricity hadn't done more than blip once when the planta came on line. The air conditioner hummed and the refrigerator made ice.

When I arrived at their doors people were pleased to see me, though we didn't know each other. I didn't understand Italian or Portuguese or a couple other languages I heard but they all seemed clear that if a pot-bellied Americano appeared in their doorway humming, dancing, and miming the act of drinking then he was inviting you to a party. Their eyes lit up and within less than half an hour two dozen people crammed our suite.

One floor above, the hurricane had found its way into the building through the laundry and swept away washers and dryers, overturned steel shelving and smashed paint cans that mixed with hundreds of gallons of water, cascading in ankle-deep waterfalls down the main staircase. When I arrived back at the suite my feet were painted white almost like a pair of socks and the now fully inebriated German proprietor was lurching upstairs toward the new disaster.

Less than an hour later the music stopped, dancers stood motionless and the room grew deathly quiet. The wind had spent itself and we heard nothing but a distant dripping and the reassuring hum of the refrigerator. "The eye?" someone said.

They say you'll see blue sky in the eye of a hurricane but leaning out over the balcony railing I felt dizzy and focused instead on what remained of Santo Domingo, a city of three million people. Earlier we watched satellite dishes take flight like saucers, radio towers

lean and crumple, trees uproot, but now this was a different thing.
The baseball stadium to our south, a steel structure, was littered toy-
like across a block of homes. The apartment building south of us
had no windows and no frames to hold them, the rectangular black
holes made them seem as if they'd been abandoned for decades.
Water was standing everywhere and the streets were gone. The city
was a city no more.

Below, our own street was hidden by fallen trees and debris. My
rental van was still there, untouched. Winding its way through the
disaster, flashers bright against the spinning twilight sky, a taxi
moved slowly along. Duct-tapped to its rear window the number
was 65. Sammy had hit another one.

The banshee wind returned and the party resumed.

I was pouring ice into Victor's scotch, about to do the same for the
two friends he'd brought along, when the telephone rang. Again I
was amazed this could happen at the height of the storm.

"Hello."

"What's the matter with you?"

"Ah, Riña."

"How can you be so stupid? I'm surprised you're not dead."

"I'm surprised the phones are working."

There was a pause and our connection was so good I heard her
breathing. Then she said, "What's that noise? Sounds like a party."

"It is a party. We got plenty of food left and people brought
enough booze to last a week. Come on over."

What she said sounded choked but the receiver had been slammed
loud enough to make up for it.

"Was that that dumb girl again?" Patricia asked.

"She's angry about us risking our lives."

"No she's not. She's mad because we aren't giving in to her
hysterics, her overwrought need to protect and mother us even
though she isn't even dry behind the ears herself." She giggled.
"Well, I guess nobody's dry behind the ears tonight. But you know,

they hate self-sufficiency. We aren't supposed to get along without her....them."

"Who?"

"Government pukes," she said.

"How many of those rum and cokes have you had?"

That night we slept fitfully against the screaming wind, our suitcases and valuables stacked above the closets. Don had built the closets of concrete and they had concrete roofs. The speckled granite floors were awash and from time to time the rattling louvered windows were hammered until they parted slightly and sprays of water showered us, wetting our bedding, waking us yet again.

In the morning we were remarkably rested and in the stillness of the retreating hurricane we saw a city of millions reduced to ruin. The destructive aftermath more terrible then the storm.

The morning wore on with stories of bodies nearby in our street, looting and murder, a school filled with children washed into a flooding gorge drowning them all. We listened to the wailing of a single voice – whether male or female I never decided – somewhere distant, mourning in a way even the wind had not duplicated. And on the rooftop, somehow, dozens of large frogs had landed, and their croaking so out of place and confused that someone finally went up and shoveled them to their deaths.

Stories of personal tragedy came first from hotel employees who had gone home that morning but returned to work. Their homes were gone or decimated, or safe and held by armed family. The reservation's clerk returned. One wall of her house had collapsed. Her neighbors ransacked it. She found nothing worth keeping and came back to work, disillusioned and accepting the inevitable, as city dwellers often do. Later the next day I found out she didn't have enough money to eat.

We endured many strange days after that as we waited for the airport to reopen – even the concrete operations tower was heavily damaged. But that first day was a windless, battlefield quiet one, marking the end of something terrible before beginning to unearth what was more terrible.

At home there would've been the sound of chainsaws and the backup alarms of front-end loaders and heavy equipment. In Santo Domingo we heard chopping. Thousands of machetes hacking branches or striking blow after blow against giant banyans that stood since before Columbus. And above it there remained not one satellite dish, radio tower or television antennae. The German's generator hummed, and it was reassuring, but we spoke little that morning.

Later in the day we walked to the SuperColmado Maximo Gomez. It was open but dark. A woman I'd never seen before sat on a stool behind the tall counter selling canned goods off and on. Across the street we noticed activity at McDonald's.

"What's going on over there?" I asked, in my bad Spanish.

"Free food," she said.

"McDonald's?"

"They worked all night and hauled in another planta too. There's a sign up on Maximo Gomez. Been a line since early this morning." She leaned both elbows on the counter. "Hasn't done my business much good."

I turned to Patricia. "When you were upstairs during the storm we cheered as the arches blew down."

"Why?" She was genuinely puzzled.

"I don't know. Mediocrity I guess."

"What in the hell are you talking about?"

"Never mind. Think they have the drive up open too? All that free food."

She pulled one of the empty plastic chairs closer and rested her feet on it. "We've been giving free food to everybody for two hundred years. What's the matter with you?"

The golden arches were gone and the remains of a dozen royal palms stood blasted and stripped in the tiny fast food yard. The roof was littered with leaves and debris around a bright blue plastic tarp patching a hole, and three of the long yellow fluorescent lights flickered in the daylight. I heard the generators humming and there was a steady flow of cars and pedestrians. Voices drifted across the street, and laughter.

Patricia said, "I'm tired of spending my vacation sitting on the sidewalk outside a Dominican mini-mart."

"Not much else we can do."

"I want to go to the beach."

"Doubt we could even get there, and if we did won't be anything but plastic bottles and broken trees."

"Then you can clean it up."

One of my favorite photographs from that trip is of my son-in-law on a wide beach, naked to the waist, bent double straining against a heavy load of palm fronds he's dragging toward a pile at Playa Palanque. His hat has blown off and you can see the muscles in his legs flexing from the tension.

Revenge of the Schoolmasters

Tropical night breezes from the mountains rattled the copey leaves along the boulevard where Harry Penfield was hiding. Harry had planted those copey himself three years before and was astonished that he could conceal himself in their dark shadows such a short time later. He shifted the holstered .38 more toward the center of his back and listened for the sound of an engine.

Harry had decided to do this alone. If they shot back he would shoot to kill. Otherwise he would only wound them. They had egged his house four times. Rocked it twice. The last time they'd shattered the rear window of his new Jeep Wagoneer and frightened his wife and two little girls. They had escalated their attacks on him and his family and the next escalation better be his, or it might be too late. His three-year-old daughter shuddered at any sudden noise and refused to sleep alone in her room. When he walked along the high school hallways there were snickers, secret grins and farting noises behind his back. He maintained control in class but outside there was a growing tide of unrest and disrespect that couldn't be ignored or tolerated if he wanted to continue teaching. He'd complained to the administration but they did nothing. After all, the principal told him, we're all experiencing much the same. Private security was hired for administrators. Teachers were on their own. Fine, Harry thought, then I'll do it my way.

Calle Pescadores, where Harry lived, wound along a high ridge of cleared land a quarter mile above the Caribbean. His was the only occupied house, though several others were in various stages of construction. The Penfields had no close neighbors and if they cried out, no one would hear. If Harry fired the pistol it would be a distant sound and he doubted anyone would come to investigate, since in a city of several million gunshots were common enough.

A pair of headlights swung onto Calle Pescadores from the east and slid toward him. Harry crouched closer to the tree trunk, then thought better of it and stood behind it. The lights came on slowly and he withdrew the weapon. Could they see him?

The driver leaning across the empty passenger seat searching for a house number. A taxi. After it passed, Harry relaxed and holstered the .38. Maybe they weren't coming.

One of the math teachers, Otto Linder, was first to be attacked. His windows were smashed after more than two dozen threatening phone calls ordering him to leave the island, or die, a voice said. The administration shrugged it off. Harry and his best friend, Norm Chadwick, joined forces with the Linders, spending nights on their roof armed with sacks of potatoes. When the cars and light pickups finally did arrive late one night the students met a barrage of raw spuds cracking and splattering their vehicles. The next day the teachers searched the parking lots for damaged vehicles and found nothing unusual except one bent windshield wiper with a small piece of potato skin stuck to the blade. Their first clue.

The school campus was the size of a small university with acres of playing fields and ample parking facilities. It took them two days and a 100-peso bribe paid to one of the school chauffeurs to

find the car's owner – Tim Gleason, the school counselor. But that
didn't make sense. Gleason had a school car, like Norm, who was
curriculum director. Everybody liked Gleason. Why would he be
involved? Another mystery.

That weekend two high school boys climbed a tree alongside
Norm's garden wall and photographed him sunbathing in the nude.
The pictures circulated throughout the school and finally the School
Board convened a special session. Latino board members thought
the issue a complete waste of their time, just more North American
silliness. He was in his own private garden after all. The Americans
just wanted it to go away, and Ellen Ruskin, a liberal feminist who
often lectured the board on women's rights and evils of the male
sex, labeled it perversion and insisted if Norm would sunbathe nude
it was a short step from that to molesting young girls. She compared
him to Richard Nixon. The Chairman pointed out that as far as he
knew Nixon had never been photographed naked. Ms. Ruskin said it
was only a matter of time.

When the board meeting finally ended at 11:15 p.m., nothing
was decided. Norm kept his job and a reprimand was placed in
his file denouncing nudity in any form. The Board established a
policy that teachers and administrators must remain clothed at all
times. Harry later asked Norm what in the hell he'd been thinking.
Norm replied that he'd been sunbathing in the nude since he was
a boy growing up in China, the son of missionary parents. In the
East, nobody thought a damn thing about nudity and people there
could distinguish between nakedness and sex. It was only prudish
feminists that didn't know the difference and he would keep on
getting naked whenever he felt like it.

Nevertheless, Harry thought, behind his tree, the damage was
done. Once again there was fuel for the fire of unrest.

No real issue surfaced to define this unrest. Sides drawn by
personality instead of reason. Shouting, fist fights at a PTA meeting,
a fellow teacher's husband took Harry into the nurse's office to

show him a .45 automatic he planned to use on him if he didn't change sides and quit supporting Superintendent Ross Bodin.

Ross was fearless, a strong leader who insisted on academic excellence from students and faculty. But in his youth he'd contracted polio and it left him partially disabled – pigeon-toed with an odd, rolling gait, a curled hand and a peculiar, effeminate appearance. In Latino America this cost him dearly, regardless of its unfairness. Worse, he appeared vulnerable, an easy mark, though friends like Harry knew better.

That summer, someone had waited below Bodin's fifth floor apartment and attempted to shoot him through the glass patio doors. Bullets ricocheted from the ceiling and embedded themselves in a bathroom wall. No injury, but this was an important school, with children of embassy officials from many nations in attendance, even the President of the Republic's family. Police and a contingent of the local Secret Service were assigned Bodin as protection. Harry was unimpressed. More boneheads with guns.

Ross took the potato skin evidence seriously and kept a close eye on Gleason through a willing army of friends and informants, and soon uncovered the counselor's political maneuvering. He coveted Ross's job. Ross ordered surveillance of the parking lot and discovered that the potato skin car belonging to Gleason was driven mostly by his high school-age son, Todd.

On the dark boulevard, Harry decided to give it five more minutes, then go inside and get some sleep. Mountain breezes had strengthened, carrying perfumed scents of frangipani and the less delightful stench of a nearby latrine used by construction workers.

A few seconds later he heard the engine.

The vehicle showed no light. It also approached from the east. He strained his eyes to see, but it came on slowly as if making sure no one waited in ambush. He heard voices and muffled laughter. Someone said "Shut up!" in a hushed voice.

Sweat trickled along Harry's spine but he slipped the .38 from its

holster in a single smooth motion, cocking the hammer and gripping
the handle with both hands. He was deep in the shadow of the trees
and as the vehicle approached he stayed hidden. Calm resolve
enveloped him now that the moment had come. He planned to hold
his fire until they acted, then step out, level the pistol, order them to
stop, and if they fired – he was sure they were armed – he'd have no
choice.

But it didn't happen that way. A blonde head poked from the
passenger window and the voice of Tim Gleason's son, Todd, said
clearly, "Get ready! Throw when we're even with the driveway."

Harry didn't wait. He stepped out into the light of the boulevard
and took careful aim at a group of boys standing in the pickup bed
armed with rocks and sling-shots. The hammer was back and he
coldly notched the front sight, slid his forefinger onto the trigger and
squeezed.

What happened next was never clear to Harry, though he thought
about it often, replayed it, regretted it. He had taken his finger off
the trigger and let them pass. Aloud, he said, "I can't shoot any
kids."

They'd seen him standing there and roared away so fast several
boys fell and one nearly catapulted out onto the street. By then
Harry was in the street and had himself lined up again, and again he
couldn't fire the weapon, not even to shoot in the air as a warning.
It was less than a decade since Harry returned from the war, where
he had never hesitated. Not even once. He thought maybe he had
become a coward, or grown up, seen enough violence, or had
somehow come to believe in turning the other cheek.

Harry Penfield lowered the hammer, replaced the pistol in its
holster, went inside and slept soundly.

The next day was Friday, and payday. By tradition, Harry, Norm,
and Superintendent Bodin left campus by 3 p.m. and met later at
Refugio, an obscure bar on the outskirts of the city where they
were unlikely to encounter anyone they knew. There they discussed

happenings at school, hashed over the gossip of the small expat community and spent some of their pesos on cold Presidente and chicharrones de pollo.

Harry had Seventh Period free that semester and that gave him fifty minutes to confront Todd Gleason before leaving to meet Norm and Ross. He couldn't shoot the boy but he could chew his ass. Maybe even scare him enough to put a stop to all the nonsense.

Harry persuaded Norm to call Gleason out of class and into his office, where they could be alone. Todd was wary after Norm left, closing the door. His eyes flashed round the small room but his mouth remained a tight line, his jaw muscles flexing with rhythmic tension.

"So, what was all that about last night?" Harry asked.

"All what?"

"Rocks, slingshots, eggs, coming by my house. All that."

Gleason made a sort of snot-sucking noise through his nose, sneered and said, "Well now Mr. Penfield, I'm sure I don't know what you're talking about."

"Todd. I saw you."

"Yeah? Maybe you were drunk. Did you ever think of that?"

Harry forced a smile and leaned back in Norm's chair. "You know Todd, there's really only one way this can end."

"Yeah? You leaving?"

"No, Todd. I'm not going anywhere. What I'm talking about here is violence. It escalates until somebody gets hurt, or worse."

"If you're scared, Sir. Go home."

"I am home, Todd. And plan to stay until long after you're gone. So you need to think about the consequences of what you are doing. I mean the consequences to yourself."

Todd snickered. "What's that? A kinda threat?" Using both hands, he swept the dirty blonde hair from his eyes. "Just because you're a teacher, you can't threaten me."

"Sure I can." Harry's smile widened again. "And much more, if this keeps up."

"Wait 'till I tell my dad you're threatening me. He's your boss. He'll fire you."

"He's not anybody's boss. He's a counselor. You might remind him of that. And if anybody's likely to be fired, it's probably him, if it turns out he's pulling your strings and undermining the administration."

Todd's face reddened. "Screw you Penfield."

Harry stood and leaned forward. "You know Todd, in my experience there's really nothing on earth quite as stupid as a sixteen-year-old punk like you. The next time you come around my house I might not hold my fire, but put a .38 special round right through the side of your empty head. Now that Todd, is a threat. If I were you, I'd go tell my daddy to start packing. It's time you'all got your worthless asses back to Alabama. Now get out of my sight."

Todd Gleason's eyes widened with hatred, and his mouth curled like a bent sword. "I'll get you, Penfield. You pussy."

Todd slammed out of the room and Harry blew a long sigh. He'd gone too far, he thought. But at least he'd put some pressure on the opposition. An offensive act, even if it fails, creates wariness in an enemy. A defensive position, no matter how strong, is still a defensive position. If nothing else, Todd Gleason knew they weren't afraid and there was a possibility of retaliation. By the look on his face, Harry guessed the boy, and maybe his father too, had believed this would be an easy thing. Harry grinned to himself and thought, Ross is going to kill me.

An hour later, Harry sat down heavily behind the wheel of his Jeep Wagoneer. The seat burning hot. His rear window still covered in cardboard from a box he'd carved up. His mechanic couldn't find a rear window for a 1972 Jeep Wagoneer. It would have to be flown in from the States at considerable expense. But that wasn't as depressing as another afternoon with Bodin and Norm. They had a two-decade history. Bodin, once principal of an American Singapore

school, had fired Norm on some whim of the board, and felt guilty
enough to hire him here to make up for it. So Harry feared that
Bodin was not only over his guilt complex, but would revert to his
rather caustic nature and belittle Norm for the nudity incident that
every student, teacher, and board member was now gossiping about.
It would no doubt prove to be a tiresome evening.

The vehicle started well enough. Harry had wired the hood closed
as a precaution against stink bombs. Two other teachers hadn't
been quite so lucky. One had exploded in the O'Briens' car and
frightened their children into hysterics. Their mother fainted and
O'Brien jumped out and stood in the faculty parking lot evoking
all manner of evil and misfortune upon whomever was responsible.
All this at the top of his lungs, to the amusement of the student
body and even some of the faculty. Except Janet Hill, who taught
junior high social studies. Janet was first to be bombed, and after a
couple Cuba Libres, blubbered about her never-ending fear and the
embarrassment of having peed down her leg. Harry backed from his
parking slot.

Refugio was a dump. Nothing to indicate it was even a bar, except
the broken Presidente beer sign that dangled by one stubborn angle
iron from the rusted steel eave of the roof. Locals drank there, and
after some time had come to accept the Americans. They nodded
politely, knowing that Juanito, who owned the place, had enough
sense to charge them twice the price. The Americans understood
that, but were pleased that twice the price at Refugio was half
price anywhere else. Harry hid his vehicle behind the building in a
chicken yard and went inside, waiting alone at their usual table by
the shaded window.

Norm arrived driving his giant white Ford LTD station wagon.
Then Bodin in his chauffeured Lincoln Town Car, also white with
black velvet curtains covering its rear window. The first words out
of Bodin's mouth when they were seated came out as Harry had
expected. "So, Mr. Chadwick. I had no idea you were a nudist."

Norm liked Bodin, but feared him. Losing his job those years past,
being forced to move to Japan, were never far from his thoughts
when he talked with the Superintendent. It was difficult to call him
Ross, and be at ease. So Norm answered with a denial. "I'm not a
nudist."

"What do you call it then when you run around naked?"

"Sunbathing."

Ross Bodin had a mocking way of rolling his eyes and pursing his
lips that registered equally with student or faculty. The schoolmaster
enduring the antics of a dumb kid. "Well, whatever *you* call it Mr.
Chadwick, it made a fine mess for all of us. One more reason to
believe we are incompetent and foolish."

Harry often defended Norm to Bodin and feared that Bodin was
tiring of it. He jumped in anyway. "Ross, this thing has nothing
to do with Norm and you know it. If you're right about Gleason
campaigning for your job, he'll spread rumors, harass anybody who
sticks up for you."

Ross shrugged. "True enough," he said. "But aren't we damn fools
to provide the ammunition for him?"

Norm's face reddened. "I have an eight-foot solid concrete wall
around my property. How was I supposed to guess some dumb kids
would climb it and photograph me taking the sun?"

"You were supposed to have enough sense to keep your clothes on
in the first place!" Ross said.

"We're all on edge," Harry said. "I did something last night much
worse than sunbathing in the nude. I nearly shot Gleason's asshole
of a kid. So his son is involved. I saw his face, his long dirty blonde
hair, and heard his voice. But I was waiting, I had them in my
sights, I just couldn't fire."

Both men were silent. The waiter arrived with their beer and
barbecued chicken. They waited until he departed before Ross said,
"I didn't know you had a weapon. But you did the right thing."

"My wife doesn't think so."

"Scared for the children."

"Of course. So am I, and next time I might blow their punkass heads off." Here Harry paused and took a deep breath. "Even worse," he continued, "an hour ago I told Todd that."

"Told him what?" Ross asked.

"Told him I might blow his stupid head off next time."

"An hour ago?"

"In Norm's office. Got him in there, shut the door and gave him a good old-fashioned ass-chewing. Scared him, too. At least now he knows we're done being victims. Told him to take that message to his dad."

Ross Bodin was a tall man. Six-foot-four. He leaned back in his chair, steepled his long fingers and nodded slowly. "I guess it's time."

"Time?" Harry said, expecting to get fired.

"I've been pressuring the board to provide security for some of you who have been vocal in support of the administration and the school," he said. "It won't hurt to tell them this story. They will know you are armed and if they don't do something we may soon have a tragedy on our hands. People can be pushed only so far." He paused to pour his beer and take a long drink. "I shouldn't tell you this and you better not repeat it. Understood?" They nodded. "A colonel in the Secret Service called me into his office yesterday. Two arrests have been made. Locals who have students with us. Both had made threats against the school and were found carrying firearms. More important, they believe now that Curt Farrow fired the shots at me, not Gleason or his bunch."

Harry's mouth dropped open. "The Principal?"

"Yes," Ross said. "And his wife."

"I'm going home to the States," Norm said.

Ross smiled. "You don't have a home."

"I know. But if I did I'd go there."

Harry stared hard at his boss. "You're telling us that the locals are armed but the Americans are doing the violence?"

"Seems so."

"Well, they should arrest the damned Americans then!"

"You know better then that. We keep this place afloat, even if there aren't a majority of American students anymore. We need to be smart."

Norm studied his beer. "His wife? Lucy? She's like, from Iowa."

"Well," Ross said, "she covered for him. They caught her in a lie about where they were the night I was shot at, and principal or not, you know that Farrow owns a house full of guns. He has the means."

Norm looked up. "There's that rumor about a guy he killed in Honduras. I never believed it, but…."

"He has a violent temper," Harry said. "I saw him punch a taxi driver on the Malecón once."

"Convenient for me," Ross said with a grin. "I've wanted to be rid of him for some time. Now I have the justification."

"I don't understand this," Harry said. "None of it makes sense."

Ross smiled at him. "Seen it before, when I was young like you. First assignment overseas I taught at a mining school in the Ecuadorian mountains. We were isolated. About 150 miners, teachers, local laborers and their wives. Everybody was fighting or screwing everybody else. Tension grew and the whole place almost blew up. I was ready to quit teaching after that." He rotated his bottle and stared awhile at the damp napkin beneath it. "This is bigger, more violent, but it's like that. A battle. War. Our job is to find the leaders and get rid of them. Once that's done, everything will calm down."

Harry remembered then the story Ross once told him about Vietnam. When he was Principal in Singapore he became interested in the war and wanted to see it. Through military contacts at school he managed a flight to DaNang for a long weekend. Harry was unduly angered when Ross told how he'd stayed at a downtown hotel and dined by candlelight on the rooftop, protected by a parapet of sandbags. The food was excellent, he'd claimed, and the view of the war spectacular. Lots of star shells and tracers, like fireflies in the night. Orange explosions on the outskirts of the city. Harry realized from the dates, that he'd been there that night, fighting, while Ross sat on a rooftop sipping his Tía María, enjoying the show.

Ross Bodin was not like other men Harry knew. He reveled in controversy and political intrigue, even war. Harry doubted Bodin would lift a hand against anyone. His weapons were intellect and subterfuge and cunning. There was no doubt in Harry's mind that Ross Bodin was a thoroughly dangerous man.

"These bastards," Harry said. "I left home because of them. Burning the cities, or rotting them. I came home from war and fought a worse one on campus. Had to get out." He drank the remainder of his beer in one gurgling string of swallows. "It starts again now, I'm not going anywhere. It ends here for me."

"I'll drink to that," Norm said.

Ross stood. "I can't stay. I have a meeting." He smiled. "Now you boys behave, and don't drink too much." He signaled his chauffeur, who brought the car around.

When he'd gone, Norm said, "Let's get drunk."

This wasn't an easy task, since both men held their liquor rather well, but it appealed to Norm because he'd been humiliated, and each day faced classrooms filled with students that had seen him naked. And Harry, well, he was just tired. At 31, he'd managed to survive jungle war and urban war, suicide bombers and hippies. He'd found a tropical island and brought his family there to safety, and found instead another war, so silly and pointless that he couldn't imagine there was enough beer or rum on the island to close his mind to it.

Four hours later they were too drunk to drive home. Refugio served hors d'oeuvres but no meals. They were forced into the dark street. In this part of the city electricity was rare. People cooked over open fires, drank their rum warm, ate with their fingers, laughed, shouted, danced and made love. They walked among them and felt more at home with such people and in such surroundings then they did with their own countrymen. And they found food, and ate, and sobered up a little.

"I love this goddamned place," Norm said.

"It does have heart."

"More then that." Norm sat resting his back against a palm in a common yard, people nearby enjoying the evening and making no fuss over them, or excluding them either. "My butt's full of sand," he continued. "Do you know what would happen if I took my pants off right now and shook them out?"

"Norm! If you don't get off this nudity shit," Harry said, "I'm going to kick your sandy ass myself."

"Big talker," Norm said. "I just meant these people don't care. They're normal. We're the ones who are abnormal. That's all. We're freaks."

Warm banks of blue smoke drifted beneath the palms, carrying smells of barbecue sauces and charcoal. Harry felt better after he'd eaten and now he wanted some rum. They sold pints of rum here in round bottles with yellow netting and people drank it like soda, and it was good rum, too.

Harry asked, "Did you mean that before? About going home?"

"I guess not," Norm answered.

"I'm never going home," Harry said. "Two years ago we shipped everything we own down from the States. Jenny, our three-year-old, was born here. She's a citizen and she can't sleep at night because some asshole is terrifying her in what is really her own country. We need to drive them out. To get them, just like Ross said."

"Then let's do it."

"How?"

"Well," Norm said. "I guess you couldn't kill them."

"Could you?"

"No."

"Then what?"

Norm stood and stretched his back. "We'll meet at your place and talk it over. Make a plan."

"It's almost midnight."

Norm shrugged. "The night is young."

They drove separately to Harry's place. Traffic was light in the city, and Harry, bottle by his side, became fascinated by his headlights - a way he sometimes measured the foreignness of the place. Air so thick it dimmed the headlights of cars and trucks. An amazing thing for air to do - absorb light like deep water absorbs color, washing it to colorless gray. A phenomenon that removed Harry from all he'd known, across this wide sea to a place where even the air you breathe is something to savor as foreign and remarkable.

Anita, his wife, thought it an odd observation when he first mentioned it years ago. "Yeah. So?" she said. "It's the tropics. Humidity? Get it? No big deal."

Anita was a practical woman and not curious. She liked clarity in her life so she could put things in their place and move on. When she'd discovered that rats liked coconut she never sat under another palm tree. Harry, fascinated by the incongruity, thought he might write a novel someday and title it *There's a Rat in Every Palm Tree*. What an eye-opener.

He eased the Jeep into his carport and cut the engine. It was late and Anita would be in bed. A light sleeper, he feared she'd wake up and raise hell with him, and Norm too.

A few minutes later, when Norm arrived and they were hushing each other on the front balcony of the house and keeping a sharp eye on the street, Anita did appear barefooted in a long white nightgown made of some slinky material. "Do you boys have any idea what time it is?" she asked.

"Probably around midnight," Harry said.

"No. 1:15 a.m."

"Oh."

She stared at Norm and back to Harry. "You're drunk."

"We're not drunk," Harry assured her. "We had a couple drinks after work."

"It's ten hours after work."

"She's right," Norm said. "It is ten hours after work."

Harry sighed. "Norm, shut up. You're not helping."

"I'm just agreeing."

"Don't agree. Just shut up."

Anita came closer, trying to see their faces in the dark. "How drunk are you?"

"We're just tired," Harry said. "We've been hashing things over. Now that you mention it, we could use a drink. So, while you're up."

Anita spun around and the slap of her bare feet on the granite floor faded as she disappeared into the darkened house.

"Okay," Harry said. "Let's talk it over. What's on your mind?"

"I'm fifty-six years old," Norm announced. "This is probably my last job overseas, or anywhere else. I've got a rental house in New York, a half decent savings, and still play a mean game of tennis. This is it for me. After all these years I finally made it into administration and a good salary. Some jackass redneck son-of-a-bitch and his arrogant punk kid are not derailing the rest of my life. I won't have it. Hear me? I just won't."

It was funny, Harry thought. He never really considered the age difference. Norm was at the end and Harry at the beginning. Yet, they were equal friends. Norm didn't preach or lecture him, and physically Norm was a match for anyone. He did play a mean game of tennis and Harry had yet to beat him. His serve was frightening and Harry couldn't return one in ten. But the real depth of their friendship grew from something intangible. In their deeper moments they found in each other kindred spirits. Life had its mysteries for them both but both handled it in much the same way, through wry humor most days and melancholy in the bad times. Both men buoyed up under pressure, and neither collapsed. So Harry knew they were going to do something. Not just drink, talk, blow off steam. And it sobered him a little.

"Did you have a plan?" he asked.

"Kind of. Where the hell is your wife with the drinks?"

"Probably went back to bed."

"I should've," she said from the shadows, stepping out with a wooden tray loaded with three Cuba Libres, a bottle of Burmudez, limes and Coca Cola. "But after all, I'm only a woman and accustomed to being exploited."

"Are you joining us?" Harry asked, noticing the three glasses.

"Damn right," she said. "I'm tired of slinking around in this house. It's time you boys put an end to all this nonsense."

"Well," Harry began, "that's exactly what we're here to talk about. Norm has a plan."

"Let's hear it," she said.

"It's not a plan really. An idea," Norm said.

"Okay. What?" Anita asked.

Norm sipped his drink, squirmed in his iron rocker, moving it more rapidly. "Well, it's complicated because this whole thing is complicated. It has sort of an energy of its own now, like some unidentifiable locomotion, you know? We can't see the engine that drives it. We just know it's out of control and effects us all."

Anita curled her feet up under her nightgown to keep them off the cool granite tile. "You aren't as dumb as you look Norm. But I'm tired of waiting. I'm scared for the girls. These people, even if they're hard to pin down, are making all the moves and we just react or defend or accept. We can't keep doing that. I can't."

Harry agreed. "She's right. If we keep doing nothing, it's going to escalate all the more until it's completely out of control. So come on, what's the plan?"

"It's that Gleason kid," Norm said. "He's the key. I doubt his dad even put him up to it, just feeds his hatred of us and looks the other way. I mean, he must know what little Todd boy is up to, but figures what can we do? You couldn't shoot him. I couldn't."

"I could," Anita said.

"We've got to take him out somehow," Norm continued. "We got to."

"How?" Harry asked.

"Grab him," Norm answered.

Anita and Harry stared at him. "By that you mean what?" Anita asked.

"I mean grab him. Take him. Scare hell out of him. He's got to be alone sometime. We can wear masks."

Anita said, "I take that back about you not being as dumb as you look. For crying out loud. Masks? Are you the Ku Klux Klan? And what would you do with him once you got him?"

"Beat the shit out of him," Norm said.

Harry nodded. "I like that idea."

"You're both crazy," Anita proclaimed. "You'll end up in jail, fired from your jobs, probably deported."

"Be fun though," her husband said.

"I know," Anita replied. "There's nothing like a good kidnapping and aggravated assault to give you a lift." She stared at Norm. "When were you planning to do this?"

"Tonight."

"So, like right now?"

"Well, we can have another drink first."

Anita wasted no time in mixing them, hoping they would both get drunk enough to pass out and forget the kidnapping plan. Why were men so like boys? She stiffened their drinks with two shots and handed them out. "This isn't the night for it," she said, smiling. "Take some time over the next couple days to draw up a sensible plan of action. Something well-thought out enough to put an end to all the craziness. Can't you do that?"

Harry was not fooled. Sipped his drink and smiled at her. "You're right," he said. "If we make a more complete plan we might get them all. One overwhelming attack. A blitzkrieg. Right Norm? We can do that."

Norm was thrown by the sudden change in tactics. "You mean we're not going to snatch that punk after we finish this drink?"

"Oh, we might still snatch him. But not tonight."

"Why not?"

"Because it will take two of us, and I'm not going with you. I think Anita's right. We need a better plan."

Norm leaned forward in his chair, giving Harry a hard look with bloodshot eyes. "Well, that ain't too friendly."

Harry just smiled at him. They talked about revenge instead of tactics and all three agreed that punishment was not always revenge, but could be. There had to be punishment or nobody was safe from anybody and Norm told a couple stories to illustrate the point. Anita mixed them another strong insurance drink before going back to bed and leaving them alone.

When she'd gone, Harry said, "We move tonight."

"Kidnap the bastard?"

"No," Harry said, smiling. "I got a better idea. Give him a large dose of his own medicine. Scare the piss out of him and his folks too. Get 'em all and hit 'em hard!"

"But not kidnap him?"

"Remember where the Gleasons live?"

"Sure," Norm said. "We've done parties there. Along Mirador Park in that fancy glass apartment complex. Best address in town."

"Did you hear what you just said? Glass. Not just a little glass but glass four stories high on both sides of every apartment. Glass facing the mountains and glass facing the sea and the park. Only thing holding that building up is glass. Get me?"

Norm gulped a satisfying amount of rum and grinned. "Glass," he said. "Man, can you imagine it?" He wagged his head. "But it won't work."

"Why not?"

"Because the whole damn place is patrolled by armed security. It's a fortress. Lit up like a baseball stadium. These guys are armed with shotguns and pistols. We can't stand around there throwing rocks or whatever you've got in your head. We'd be dead or apprehended in two minutes."

Harry mulled this over awhile and said, "I'm hungry. Let's eat."

"What you got?"

"Cold fish and plantain chips."

"What kinda fish?"

"Grouper."

"Okay. It doesn't have the eyes in it does it?"

"No. It's just fillets."

After Harry came back with two large plates, they ate in silence. Harry thought the fish tasted a little old and tried to remember what day they'd fried it up. A week ago at least, he thought. Well, it was cooked. You can't get sick from something that's been cooked even if you eat it a month later.

"Have you seen those guys who patrol the place?" he asked Norm. "I mean, how do they work?"

"Well," he said, spitting fish skin onto his plate, "I never studied them or anything. Just watched them walk around the complex with their guns. Kind of an odd sight at a party, you know? I was just curious."

"How many were there?"

Norm shrugged. "I don't know. One or two maybe."

Harry thought this over awhile. "Then there's got to be a time – some minutes – when neither of them is nearby Gleason's place, right?"

"I guess."

"So we go there. We watch awhile, see how they do it."

Norm said, "But what are we going to do?"

"We're going to find one hell of a big rock, like a bowling ball, and slam that baby right through all that beautiful glass."

Norm gnawed one of the hard, cold plantain rounds. "Do you have any ketchup?"

"Did you hear what I said?"

"I heard. Does that mean I can't have any ketchup? These plantain should've been heated. I can taste the peanut oil. I need some ketchup."

Harry retrieved the ketchup. "Okay. Now. What do you think?"

Norm pounded the bottom of the bottle with the heel of his hand, plopping a slough of ketchup onto his plantain. "Yeah," he said. "But where you gonna get a rock that big?"

"Right down the street," Harry said, clearly pleased with himself. "Right down the street. This place is a construction zone and there's rocks like that all over. I bet we can even find a nice fat round one. And I'm going to throw that baby right through Gleason's glass house." He laughed. "People who live in glass houses shouldn't throw stones."

"Funny," Norm said. "Only one thing wrong with that plan. You aren't throwing it. I am."

"Oh?"

"Oh. Nobody laughs at my naked ass and gets by with it. I throw the rock."

"Then who drives the getaway car?"

"You. Maybe we should take your car. Everybody knows mine. It's a school car, after all."

"And they won't know mine with a back window busted out?"

"Doesn't matter," Norm said. "Use my car then. We'll do it and disappear before anybody even sees the car or us or knows what happened."

Night air had cooled just enough to form a thin mist of fog. It wet the buildings, dampened the royal palms along Mirador Parkway, and coated the rich grass with a silver sheen of reflected light from the remaining streetlights. Most had been doused to save energy, and from the high street behind the Mirador complex, Harry and Norm were encouraged by the semi-darkness.

"Bless the energy crisis," Norm said.

Harry had parked Norm's giant white station wagon in the darkest area he could find along the street. The apartment complex faced Mirador Parkway, the park itself, and the sea, no more than a quarter mile distant. They were on the street running along behind the complex – a narrow and less traveled access road. It was darker and safer there but more than twenty feet above the complex and half a block away. Norm would be forced to carry the rock, and it was the size of a bowling ball, down the incline, then across the flat expanse of lawn before getting into range for his throw.

Harry was worried. "Norm. Think this over. If you avoid the guards, how will you get all the way back up here once everybody's awake and coming after you?"

"Run."

"Carrying that belly of yours?"

"Can't very well leave it behind."

"It's not too late. Give me the rock. I'm fast Norm. I can hit that glass wall and be half way back before anybody knows what's happening. Don't be stubborn."

Norm was in the passenger seat with the rock on his lap. "Harry. I'm going to do this. I have to do this. Can't you understand that?" He stared hard at Harry. "I don't give a damn if they shoot me. It's better then not doing what I just have to do. What needs to be done."

"We're dead," Harry said. "Where are the stupid guards anyway? We've been here half an hour."

They studied the grounds, searched the shadows.

"There," Norm pointed. "At the corner of Gleason's building. See the cigarette glow? Been standing there all along I bet."

Harry could just make out a man's silhouette but saw no evidence of a weapon. A moment later the guard flipped the butt onto the grass and picked up a shotgun he'd leaned against the concrete corner of the building. "Here he comes," Harry said in a hushed voice.

The guard wore a blue uniform, light shirt and darker trousers. A peaked cap. He slung the shotgun and moved toward the west end of the complex, furthest from Gleason's.

"A minute for him to get clear," Norm said. "Then I go."

It was the longest minute of Harry's life, and thirty years later he'd remember how it felt as if it had happened just the night before.

Then Norm eased the door open, turning on the dome light, a beacon of white on the grass, reflecting in the window they were hoping to smash. "Close the door!" Harry hissed.

Norm stumbled out and slammed it in haste. Harry stared at the retreating guard's back. The guy kept moving away. Either deaf, or an idiot, Harry thought. Then, how odd was the sound of a car door in a city? He exhaled and leaned his head back on the seat to regain his composure.

When he turned to look for Norm he couldn't see him. He moved to the passenger's seat and rolled down the window. Norm was spread-eagled on the wet grass half way down the hill, flat on his back and struggling to recover the rock which had rolled downhill at least a body length away.

With the window down, the 460 cubic foot engine sounded like a NASCAR final lap. Harry switched it off and sighed into the silence. How many mistakes were they going to be allowed anyway?

Norm had made it to the bottom of the hill and was creeping forward toward the towering sheet of glass. "Go Norm, go!" Harry whispered. It was then he noticed Norm's attire – red, white, and blue checkered double-knit trousers held in place with a three inch wide white patent leather belt. Patent leather white bucks on his feet. His shirt a solid and brilliant blue. The man was dressed like a clown instead of a ninja. At least there would be no doubt in the minds of witnesses. "Go Norm!" Harry said aloud.

Norm reached what seemed to Harry a good distance for the throw. He had the rock, but just stood there. Was he chickening out? No. He was judging the distance. He moved closer, holding the rock with both hands, slowly bringing it up above his head. He staggered. The rock threw him off balance and Norm collapsed on his back again. Harry covered his eyes. He was too drunk to throw.

When he looked up, Norm had regained his footing. Feet braced wide apart, and again hefting the rock above his head, he seemed to stagger forward, and then Harry watched the rock arching into the air with incredible force, its trajectory unimaginably high as if it came from a catapult.

To Harry, time seemed suspended, the rock spinning in the night air like some slow motion meteorite, and when it collided with the glass sheet it was at least twelve feet above the ground. The glass tower shattered and the sound of it echoed like cannon fire and Harry felt the vibrations as sound waves spread across the night. He stared in disbelief. A human head rose into the air just below the disintegrating window and emitted a piercing, almost feminine scream. Todd boy. He must've come home late and slept on the couch below the window. The rock continued on through the living room, dining area and kitchen. Harry heard the smashing of tables and secondary explosions of more interior glass objects, followed by a thunderous roar as the missile connected with kitchen chairs and dishes, pots, pans, knick-knacks. Finally, it came down onto the granite floor, bounced once and exited the apartment through the sea side sheet of glass, which must've been struck very low, but collapsed nonetheless with another resounding cannonade.

Norm hadn't moved. Both he and Harry heard Todd boy's sobbing clearly in the silent aftermath. It was a sound to warm their hearts but Harry recovered his senses and screamed at Norm to move. To run.

And Norm did run. He made it half way up the hill before he fell the first time. It knocked the wind out of him, forcing him to wait on his knees until his breath came back. A few feet later he slipped on the mist-laden grass and fell again, harder.

"Damn it!" Harry bellowed at him. "Crawl! Move, move!"

The soles of Norms white bucks were slick. He slipped them off, stuffed them down his pants and struggled on in his stocking feet, barely making headway against the slope of the hill.

Harry spotted the guard, shotgun at the ready, running toward the scene, but on the opposite side of the complex where he must've heard the final sound as the rock exited.

Norm reached the door handle, jerked it open and dropped inside the station wagon just as Harry moved back behind the steering wheel. He'd forgotten to re-start the engine and fumbled to turn the key. The big engine whined and hesitated. The starter ground but failed to catch. Harry swore, panic-stricken.

"You're flooding it, Harry!" Norm shouted. "Get your foot off the gas."

Harry obeyed but the engine seemed no closer to starting.

"Relax," Norm said. "Give it a few seconds. Just relax. Quit grinding it. Distributor gets a little damp sometimes in this climate. It'll start."

And it did, finally, though Harry felt he'd aged fifty years. He punched the accelerator, the tires burned and they left the scene in a cloud of smoking rubber and high-pitched squealing. NASCAR II, Harry thought. There couldn't be a single person left asleep in the entire city and when the police began their investigation in a few hours witnesses by the thousands would come forward to give a perfect description of car, driver, and rock-throwing clown. By noon they'd be in jail and by Monday unemployed.

But they had done it.

When Monday came Mrs. Timothy Gleason and her son Todd were no longer on the island, and at 8 o'clock that morning the school's counselor himself resigned his post and tacked up a sign in the administrative offices announcing a quick sale of all his personal belongings. Discount prices. This was no comfort to Harry Penfield and Norm Chadwick, who both, sober gentlemen, waited throughout the day for the other shoe to drop. They didn't dare speak to one another.

Harry noticed a change in the atmosphere. Students whispered and he saw furtive side-long glances, but no outright disrespectful or belligerent behavior. The halls were quiet. Classes marched in near perfect cadence throughout the day and when Seventh Period came, Harry stopped by the administrative building to check his mail on the way to the teacher's lounge.

"Mr. Penfield," Ross Bodin addressed him from behind. "Would you step into my office for a moment, please?"

And so, Harry thought, this is how it will end, not with a bang but a whimper. He followed Ross into his spacious office. "Close the door," Ross said pleasantly.

Harry complied, deciding right then to confess rather then have Ross drag it out of him. "About Friday night," he began.

"So!" Ross jumped in. "You've heard. Well, I guess everyone knows by now. Poor Gleason was attacked. Viciously. Todd was nearly killed. The damage estimates to their apartment are said to be nearly twenty thousand dollars and the rental company is holding them liable for the entire amount since insurance isn't covering it. Some riot exclusion clause. Gleason got his family out this weekend and says he'll get out himself one way or another. My, what a mess." Ross grinned. "On the other hand...."

Harry didn't know what to do. What to say. Ross seemed oblivious. Finally he asked, "So who's responsible for this so-called attack?"

Ross shook his head, still grinning. "Well, I had thought it was you. At least you were one of my suspects." He smiled more broadly. "But I doubt you'd risk it. And the guards at the complex reported it was a gang. That they were overwhelmed and lucky to have escaped with their lives. So I don't suppose you have a gang, do you Mr. Penfield?"

Harry attempted a smile. "If I did," he said, "I would've turned them loose long ago."

"The board will meet in special session this evening and I'm announcing my intent to fire Principal Farrow too, and ask for their support. We'll have a clean sweep then and things should calm down. Maybe I'll move Norm up to principal. What do you think?"

"Great idea," Harry said.

"Yes, well I knew you'd say that of course," Ross said. "Loyalty is fine, but you really are rather predictable. Don't you ever do anything that's just a bit daring?"

"No," Harry said, straight-faced. "Not if I can help it. Life is exciting enough without stirring up trouble."

Nearly thirty years passed and Harry Penfield's Caribbean dreams had faded long before. He'd gone home to Michigan. And one day a mutual friend wrote him to say Norm Chadwick died in Florida. Heart attack. Ross Bodin had retired in Florida too, and was still living in a gated community there. They'd exchanged Christmas cards through the years. Called on the phone. Harry thought how silly it had been to keep the secret all this time, when it couldn't possibly matter to anyone now.

Anyway, they'd all drifted apart as people do who no longer work together or live close. But that day, after he'd lain his friend's letter aside, he felt a surge of nostalgia and it swept aside the concerns of the moment. His eyes lost their focus and he drifted.

He surprised himself when he asked directory assistance to dial

Ross Bodin's number. On the answering machine Ross's voice seemed weaker, maybe more hesitant, but Harry left a cute message and hung up. When Ross returned the call they arranged to meet in New Orleans that winter, during a reunion of former overseas school administrators.

It was January. Cold in New Orleans. A brisk, wet wind swept across Lake Pontchartrain and through the narrow streets, forcing Harry and Ross to move inside the bistro where it was warm. They were two strangers – one old, the other overweight and balding. The conversation began, ended and began again. Harry thought this meeting had been a mistake.

They drank martinis. Faster then they should have, and the gin loosened their tongues.

"You heard about Norm?" Ross asked.

"Called me. Needed money. Lost everything on some deal."

Ross ordered them a third drink. "He loved 'get rich' schemes. Had to sell his house. Tried to get me to invest in some Saudi Arabian arms deal once. So Norm. Last time I saw him he was working as a church janitor, living in a basement room. But seemed happy enough."

Harry complimented the waiter on the quality of the martinis and took a long drink of water before sipping the third one. "So many years," he mused. "Yet, like yesterday."

"The place and peculiar events," Ross said. "That's why we remember so clearly. I stayed on quite a few years after you left. Always wondered why you didn't come back."

Harry paused. Ross valued education. "Quit half way through my doctorate. Walked through the student union one day, saw a sign on the wall that said **"Newspaper Reporters Wanted" Up to $13,000 per year**. Tore it down, copied the phone number and threw the sign away. Got the job. I don't know. Guess I wanted to see if I could do what I'd been teaching all those years. Not that I've written anything brilliant or made it to the *Chicago Tribune*. Maybe English teachers are all a bunch of frustrated authors, huh?"

"Are you glad?"

"Yeah. I am. Not much money but I like going to work." Harry smiled. "Flew down here first class on my frequent flyer miles too."

Ross grinned. "I always fly first class."

"Only because Norm saved your ass."

"What?"

"Norm saved you back when the Gleason mob was after you. Don't you remember?"

"Norm didn't do anything but get naked."

Harry paused a second, then thought what the hell. "He threw a huge rock through Gleason's window and sent them packing." He saw the doubt in Ross's eyes. "He brought the vindication. We weren't an offensive force until that night. A just revenge."

"Norm? Our Norm?"

"That's the guy."

Ross gazed across the room toward the entrance as if he expected Norm to walk in. "I suspected you for awhile but never Norm. How do you know this for sure?"

"I drove the getaway car."

Ross's eyes fell among the glasses, roamed the small bread plates and leftover crumbs. His face, which had somehow survived the jowls of age, grew pinched and his eyes sagged, losing interest in what they saw. Harry sipped his drink and waited.

At length Ross said, "I knew Norm was down on his luck in Florida." He stopped talking and stared again. "I gave him a $100-dollar bill once and scolded him for wasting his money. I saw he'd lost weight, but I didn't visit him again because the neighborhood was bad and I didn't want to leave my car there, and....well, you know."

"Yeah, well," Harry said.

"Norm threw the rock?"

"Yes."

"You drove?"

"Uh huh."

"Order another drink."

Jimmy Olsen

The Missionaries

Well concealed behind the wooden louvers of the patio door, I watched from above as they climbed from the taxi and stared up at the building. Two gentlemen of the old school, wearing long sleeved white shirts yellowed with age and ironing, garters above the elbows. Heavy gear in the tropics. They nodded to one another and found the stairs. They weren't what I expected. The taller of the two wore a bow tie. His partner had stock neckwear with something on it I couldn't make out, maybe a duck. They had suspenders, dark trousers, black shoes with square capped toes. Short hair.

Saturday I spend the day at sea, diving. I was, in those early days, one of the only divers on the island. People questioned me at length about diving and rumored wrecks and the courage I displayed in shark-infested water. And I was invited to all the right parties. I wasn't pleased with uninvited guests keeping me home. I, in turn, held the maid back from her shopping.

"Llegaron Miriam," I said. They're here.

She nodded and shuffled to the door, amused by my discomfort. She'd enjoy it even more if they did ask for money. She asked often enough herself.

Missionaries eager to see me. That was a mystery. One of them - they were brothers named Harold and Albert Gustafson - had telephoned not an hour ago, asking for me by name. Albert, the caller, gave his reason for the proposed visit - a chance for them to talk to someone from home. He suggested dates for a meeting. I stalled. I was busy. Finally, he said *How about right now?* and I gave in. Just as well to get it over with if they weren't going to leave me alone. I was sure they wanted money.

The Missionaries were ushered onto the western balcony where I took my breakfast or late morning coffee in the shade. I stood as they entered and received them formally, with an edge of irritability to discourage begging. They stepped forward in single file and shook my hand. Both inclined their heads just slightly, not a bow, but a token of respect I suppose since social politeness at that time had yet to dim its lights to individual brilliance.

"Won't you sit down?" I asked, more cordially then I'd intended. "Miriam, would you bring coffee now please? Either of you like hot milk or sugar?"

"Oh, yes," Albert said. "Blonde and sweet." He chuckled at this ribaldry. It was a mallard on his tie, in flight.

It was still mid morning but I'd instructed Miriam to bring out small sandwiches, fresh fruit and sweets. Missionaries had always seemed hungry to me and both these fellows were thin, almost fragile. Their faces had an unhealthy pallor. Both were well over sixty.

The western balcony was the largest in the apartment, carefully tiled in pink granite over poured concrete with a matching solid rail, a wall of masonry troweled in circular patterns. The furniture was a bronze collection of wrought iron I'd commissioned - an assortment of small and large tables, stationary chairs and rockers. A liberal arrangement of greenery, fresh hibiscus (red, salmon, pink) displayed on three tables, the floor gleamed, no speck of dirt anywhere.

Albert Gustafson leaned back in the rocker he'd selected and asked, "What kind of a name is Bushnell?"

If they were going to put the bite on me it was a poor start. "My name," I said.

"It doesn't sound Scandinavian," Albert pressed on.

"It's not."

"Well," he said. "Minnesota. I expected, you know, most of us from that region are of Scandinavian descent. We are from North Dakota. Our mother's maiden name was Swedburg."

"The Bushnells came from the East," I explained. "Old American family. No ties to Scandinavia. Lived my early life in St. Paul."

"St. Paul," Albert mused. "That's a city."

"Yes. It's a city."

Harold wore a sort of grin but said nothing.

"Listen," I began. "Is there something I can do for you?"

"Do?" Albert asked.

"The reason for your visit."

"I explained on the telephone," he said. "We've been here a very long time, more than thirty years. Seldom speak English to anyone and don't see our own kind, you know, folks from where we came from. Got word about you from one of the third country nationals we know. All she had to say was *Minnesota*. Oh, my! Minnesota! A musical word."

"Like North Dakota?" I ventured.

"Exactly."

"Minot," I teased.

"Have you been there?"

"Sorry," I said. "Drove through North Dakota only once on I-94. I remember it was flat. Treeless."

"You have some prairie in Minnesota, too," he said. "We miss that, Harold and I. The open space. The wind. The long sky."

"I suppose."

Miriam brought coffee and sweets. The missionaries were pleased and Albert told Harold it was a wonderful spread. Harold nodded, blank-faced. I was wondering if he was mute.

"What religion are you?" I asked, making conversation.

"We're Christian," Albert explained. "Followers of Jesus Christ, you know."

"I assumed that. I mean what denomination?"

"Well," he said, sipping his blonde and sweet. "We were raised Lutheran. Mostly Lutherans there on the prairie. A few Catholics scattered about. Not many. Just a few."

"This is a Catholic country, " I pointed out. "Are you here trying to convert them?"

Harold finally spoke. "What's the matter with you? Are you crazy?"

Harold's eyes were a clear, sharp gray and set deep under thick, wild brows. I looked into them and fell silent, puzzled by his sudden hostility.

"I think what Harold means," Albert filled in, "is that people sometimes get the wrong idea about missionaries. We're not just one thing. Each mission is different."

I glared at Harold before turning my attention to Albert. "Oh," I said. "I guess I just assumed you were here to save souls and since you're Protestant you'd be wanting to save the Catholics and everybody else. There aren't many Buddhists or anything like that here. Not that I know of. We got a few Jews, I guess."

Harold had not lost his belligerence. "What do you think we've been doing here for the past thirty-three years? Eating plantain and watching the tide roll in? We know a good deal more about who's here and who's not than you do."

This wasn't going as I'd expected. "I'm not trying to insult you," I said. "I don't know anything about missionaries."

"Most people don't," Albert said in a soothing tone. "Some come here to staff churches for their denominations. Others come like Mother Teresa and minister to the poor. Some are merely accountants. One group works with birth control. Years ago a missionary, Carol Morgan, started a prestigious school here. Hospitals, orphanages, all things done by missionaries. I think Harold is concerned that you are prejudging us. Psalm-singers out haranguing people for their souls."

That was exactly what I thought. "I meant no offense," I said, staring back at Harold. "It's just that when you say things like you're followers of Jesus Christ, well, what does that really mean?"

"We're sort of like puppy dogs," Harold said. "Just trotting along behind Him with our tongues hanging out."

Albert chuckled at Harold's sardonic wit. I wanted to slap him. "I'm not very religious," I said.

"No kidding?" Harold asked. "I'd never have guessed."

"Listen here," I said. "That's my choice. It's a free country."

"Actually, it's not. But you haven't been here long enough to figure that out yet," Harold countered. "Maybe you should become a follower of the Gustafson's for awhile and we'll teach you a thing or two."

Albert was enjoying himself immensely. "Now fellows," he began. "Let's not argue religion. We came over here today for something else entirely."

"Yeah," I said. "To put the bite on me, no doubt."

"Ha!" Harold said. "You've got nothing we want."

I wanted to throw Harold from the balcony and watch him bounce. "You don't want money? Isn't that what you people always want? Money, money, money? It's the main reason I don't go to church."

"Are you poor?" Harold wanted to know.

"No, I'm not poor. I just don't see the use of handing over my hard-earned cash to somebody with their own notions of what's right and wrong, so they can go around telling others what to think." On firm ground, I settled more snugly in my chair and crossed my arms. "Most people feel the same way. You can't tell us what to think."

"Please, please," Albert begged. "We didn't come here to witness to you or ask for donations. We were just lonely for a Minnesota brogue. No more sharp words." He sipped the remainder of his coffee. "This is such good coffee, might I have a little more?"

I called Miriam.

"Please," Albert went on. "We aren't interested in soliciting from you. Our support comes from several rural congregations in North Dakota. One in northwestern Minnesota. We ask nothing of people here, except they listen to our story. We just tell the story of Jesus and people listen or not, believe or not, it's their choice as it's always been. No money."

"How can you pay the expenses for your church if you don't have money?" I asked.

Harold jumped in. "Because we're poor. We live like pigs. We have demented maniacs for disciples and they follow us through the streets screaming 'Jesus Saves! Jesus Saves!' and at night they scrawl it on trees and the sides of buildings."

Once again Albert grinned at his brother. I thought maybe it was a technique - good missionary, bad missionary. Then Albert said, "We don't have a church."

"What?"

"We don't have a church," he repeated.

"So where do you conduct services, or whatever?"

"I just told you," Harold said. "In the streets. We wander up and down. Haven't you seen us when you're driving your fancy fat American car? Little old missionary men crying out that the sky is falling?"

There really was something destructive about Harold. He hadn't taken his eyes off me for an instant and he seemed to enjoy the consequences of his prodding. I was tired of being on the defensive. "What did you do before you became missionaries?"

Harold glared at me.

"We were farmers," Albert said. "Papa died and left us almost a thousand acres of fine, rich cropland. But the Lord called us. We sold it and used the money to come here." He smiled. "Of course, that money is long gone now, and we are so thankful for the folks at home who send us a little when they can."

Here it comes at last, I thought. The bite.

"Why don't you give us a couple grand?" Harold snapped.

Albert laughed and said, "Harold!"

Since Albert insisted on treating Harold as a comedian, I persisted in taking him seriously. "Fine," I said, staring him down. "Cash? Check maybe? Made out to you personally?"

"Please," Albert said. "No more talk of money. Even jokingly. Let's not spoil our visit." He was obviously annoyed with the both of us. "Mr. Bushnell, tell us something of your work here. Shell Oil, isn't it? An underwater thing?"

"Yes." I dragged my eyes from Harold. Brawling with a missionary was probably a one-way ticket to hell. "I maintain their oil pumping station at sea - the one off Bajos de Haina. Work on the underwater pipeline to the refinery there. Weekends I'm usually out on La Caleta Bay or someplace exploring, catching a lobster for supper."

"Amazing," Albert said. "Don't you think so, Harold?"

"Most people keep their feet on the ground, if they have any sense," Harold responded.

"Well," I countered, grinning. "I make three hundred and twenty dollars an hour with my feet in a pair of fins. How much do you make, with your feet on the ground?"

"Now, now," Albert cautioned again. "Enough feet talk. I find that very interesting. How deep is the pipeline? I mean, isn't it miles off shore, at the bottom of the sea?"

"The pumping platform for the supertankers is five kilometers offshore. It's one hundred feet to the sea bed."

"Aren't you afraid of the bends? Must be terribly dangerous work even for so much money."

"Tough guy like him," Harold explained, "probably doesn't have
to worry about the bends. Immune to it. The sharks are scared of
him."

I wouldn't brawl with him, just kill him outright. "Actually, we do
see a great many sharks," I instructed. "The pumping station attracts
them and many of the fish they feed on. More than once I've had to
nudge one or pop him in the nose when he opens his mouth a little
too wide."

It didn't improve his demeanor, but Harold was quick enough to
catch my drift and seemed content finally to let me have the last
word.

Albert helped himself to another of the little sandwiches and I
noticed Miriam hovering. "Shopping," she whispered in my ear.

"Go," I said. "We'll manage."

"There's an element of danger to anything worthwhile," Albert
philosophized. "Don't you think?"

"Yes. I imagine missionarying could be fatal if you preach to the
wrong crowd," I said. I looked directly at Harold when I said it.

"Exactly," Albert said. "Exactly. *To be great is to be
misunderstood* Emerson said. A man who understood Christ, I
think. Sometimes the great story of Jesus is misunderstood." He
smiled at me. "You are afraid we want your money or to force you
to believe something our way. Take our view of things. We don't.
Nevertheless, the perceptions are sometimes dangerous as sharks.
Harold was once struck by a car on Conde. The driver shouted at
him, saying he was a gringo communist. Harold sustained three
broken ribs and his knee was dislocated. We've worked a great deal
in that part of town with the poor, you see. Some people who saw us
on the street jumped to conclusions."

"I'm sorry. I had an octopus drill a hole right through my hand
once," I said.

"Of course." Albert was a positive sort and smiled broadly.

"Carpenters strike their thumbs with hammers." He chuckled. "Or is it all nail guns now? I suppose they drill their feet to the roofs of houses." He laughed outright at the image of shingled carpenters.

"Wouldn't you be safer though," I wondered, "if you kept your opinions to yourself?"

"Wouldn't you be safer if someone else descended the depths and you stayed aboard the boat?"

"I have to make a living."

"We have a story to tell," he said. "It's not a living, but it's life. Won't you accept us?"

"I like stories myself," I said, trying to edge away from religion. "Just finished reading *Rookery Blues* by Jon Hassler. Know him? He's kind of a Catholic, I think."

"My favorite is *The Love Hunter*," Albert said. "I liked all the twists when whatshisname tries to murder his best friend with MS so he can get his wife. I don't think I've ever laughed so hard."

"He's from Minnesota, you know. Hassler, I mean."

"I met him," Albert bragged. "In Brainerd. Went to a signing there. He's very soft spoken, and broad shouldered. But that was years ago."

"Well," I said.

"We cheer for the Twins here. The island has a great baseball culture. We've been to several games. Harold loves baseball."

"Well," I said.

"I don't think we can go back home again," Albert said suddenly.

"Oh?"

"Well, I mean we do go. To visit our congregations and show slides to their mission committees, and for fund raising, but that's only a few weeks every four or five years. We don't see much but highways and church basements. And that's the best of it. The rest is shocking, like someplace really foreign. More foreign than anything here."

"Things change," I said.

"Yes," Albert nodded. "But the tractors have gotten so big."

Just like a farmer, I thought, smiling. "They cost more too."

Albert munched another sandwich before he went on. "It was the size that alarmed me because I wondered why anyone needed a machine so large. Papa farmed with horses in the beginning and then a Minneapolis Moline and finally a John Deere. These machines replaced the horse, and that was natural, but now these big machines have replaced the people. There's hardly anyone left on the land. All those large Scandinavian and German families that filled the village schools and hardware stores. I'm afraid that those big tractors are more costly than anyone imagines."

"I suppose people aren't content just to make a living from the land any longer," I said. "They want what's on TV. What everyone else wants."

"Of course. It depresses us, Mr. Bushnell. If you watch a thing change it affects you gradually, but if you go away and come back to find everything different, well then, it's like it happened all of a sudden." He drained his coffee. "I think you see it more clearly then. Abandoning the rural life is dangerous. Next to God, the land is our greatest heritage. We turn our back on it at our peril."

"That's a lot of power to put in dirt."

He nodded. "Yes," he said. "You are absolutely correct, but it's the poor families who understand this best. Without land they don't eat. We Americans I'm afraid, are so awfully fat we can't see the ground for our bellies."

Albert was beginning to get a little preachy. I wasn't going to listen to a sermon and I wasn't going to pay for it either so I stood up and lied, "I've got an appointment downtown in a little while."

Albert nodded and reached for another sandwich.

Harold stood and Albert reluctantly followed suit. "We can flag a taxi here, I'm sure," he mumbled.

"Don't bother," I said. "I'll drive you."

"We do live downtown." Albert shook his head. "But it's not the best neighborhood."

"Don't be silly. I've been across this city end to end."

I led them toward the back stairs and down to where the truck was parked.

My friend Angel had talked me into buying a Toyota pickup the year before. We all squeezed onto the bench seat. Harold sat by the window, for which I was grateful. He'd taken such an instant dislike to me. I couldn't think of any other time that had happened, at least not since high school. That's why I drove them home, I suppose. I didn't want to let it drop, have them leave with a bad taste for me, though I knew no reason to care what some old geezers from North Dakota thought.

I knew the city like the back of my hand in those days, but when Albert gave me the address I'd never even heard of the street.

"Puig Street," Albert said.

"Really? Never heard of it."

"I'll direct you."

We arrived, finally, at the end of a narrow alley. The sewers had failed and a thin persistent stream of slick gray water ran in the gutter, garbage littered the narrow, broken pavement and sidewalk. Harsh noon light and its heat had forced the residents indoors. I smelled urine and rot. I applied the brakes.

"About half way down the block," Albert instructed. "On the left. The pink one."

The street was so narrow if I stopped I'd block it, but I coasted until the wheels quit turning. Harold opened his door, stepped out and turned to me. "Why don't you come inside and see how the other half lives?" he invited.

I was curious. Harold was speaking to me again.

"By all means," Albert insisted.

"No place to park," I said.

"Oh, don't worry. People are used to going around the cars."

"Where?"

"They just drive on the sidewalk," he said. "Come in."

I didn't want to leave the Toyota. It was freshly waxed. The humble concrete facades of the squeezed houses were covered in graffiti, their faded wooden doors tight against the heat and the ladrónes, but I was curious to see their squalor.

"Take your car keys," Albert said needlessly.

Harold led the way. The building's slatted door scraped as he leaned into it. He was a little stooped and I wondered if it was from the accident. Age maybe.

We entered two steps up from the street into an airless, dim hallway. The floor was rough limestone, dull yellow but clean. A concrete staircase led up to our left but Harold stepped around it to the right and moved further back into the gloomy interior. It was surprisingly quiet. The air still and heavy. Behind the stairs Harold opened a wooden door which I'd taken to be a closet and we entered their apartment.

"Just the one room," Albert apologized. "It's cozy though, don't you think?"

"Lovely."

The three of us were forced to stand together at its center. Harold shifted back into the doorway so Albert had room enough to show me around.

"This is the kitchen," he said, pointing to a hotplate on two chipped cinder blocks balanced on a flimsy table. Beneath were piles of books and bundles of religious pamphlets and what looked to be sheet music. Hymns, no doubt. A long, reddish-brown roach sat contentedly on one of the hotplate's scored burners. "And this is the living room." Albert swept both arms around. "Over there, our library." More stacks of books and religious tracts.

"Where's the bedroom?" I asked, since the room contained no bed.

"Ah," Albert said. "The most ingenious part. Harold came up with it." He began removing pots, pans, boxes and assorted utensils from under a kind of tablecloth. "How do you like that?" he said, exposing a metal hide-a-bed with a thin mattress. "Fits crosswise when you open it up. Very functional. I sleep fine."

It was narrow. Room for one. "Where does Harold sleep?"

"There," he said, pointing outside. "Under the stairs."

Harold politely stepped aside so I could see his hide-a-bed, neatly folded and covered with a cloth similar to the one inside.

"Well," I said. "Cozy is the word."

"And a view," Albert bragged, stepping to a louvered window not much larger than a ship's porthole. It looked out into an air shaft of gray light so dusty and weak it barely reflected in the glass. "There's a little community toilet around back."

"What does something like this cost?" I had to ask.

"It's spendy," Albert said. "Fifty a month."

"Dollars?"

"Pesos."

I calculated that at the current exchange rate and it came to $37.50 per month. About one hundred dollars less than my liquor bill. "A bargain," I said.

"Señor Geraldo?" a female voice in the hall. "It is time now."

"Ah," Albert nodded. "Go ahead with her. It won't take long and I'm sure Mr. Bushnell will wait so he can say goodbye to you."

Harold abandoned the doorway and followed the voice further back into the interior.

"A baptism," Albert explained. "Infant born with spina bifida, and I'm guessing some sort of heart defect. She's dying. The mother is fourteen but wishes the child, Lucianna, to be baptized before she dies. I suppose it's the least we can do. There's no father, of course."

"Does Harold do the baptizing?" I asked.

"We believe anyone can baptize, Mr. Bushnell. Believers, I mean. There's the water, but really it's spiritual. I'm sure you were baptized yourself."

"Yes."

"Funny," he said not smiling. "You were baptized and you aren't religious."

"My parents."

"Of course," he said. "Religion seems to have so many persistent rituals practiced faithfully by so many millions of unreligious people, don't you think?"

"Give me an example, I mean other than baptism, which is something your parents usually control."

"Christmas," he said. "Easter, Passover, communion, confession, circumcision, prayer itself. Many more. A long list, I think. Maybe that's why we found a place here. This infant's mother, Dulce, has been a faithful Catholic all her life. Harold, a foreign Protestant, is baptizing her dying child. It's not religion really, but geography. Dulce's priest lives a mile or so from here in a fine rectory, and like you, has an efficient maid to care for him. Harold is here."

There didn't seem to be enough air left in the room for both of us so I stepped into the hall and said, "Well, I should be getting on."

"Just a minute. Harold will want to say goodbye, and I have something exciting to show you." He beckoned me back inside the room. "There," he said, pointing at the two-burner hot plate. "See that pan? That's my peanut-roasting pan. We make our own peanut butter!"

I caught myself before asking why they didn't buy any. "You make it?"

"Roasting the peanuts properly is the key," he said. "After that it's just mixing and stirring. We love peanut butter. Ten years without it before I made up my own recipe. Smell the pan," he said, sliding it under my nose. "Just like fresh peanuts!"

He unscrewed a mason jar and forced me to taste it. A brown paste, not unlike glue smelling of peanuts. I wondered what they gave up for it. "Listen," I began. "I get a sort of care package every week from the States. We have a parts flight and the tanker captains bring us stuff too. I mean, I've got a cupboard full of Skippy. I'll never eat it all."

Albert was pleased by the offer but shook his head. "No," he said. "We didn't want your money and we don't want your peanut butter. We just wanted to talk to you because you came from home." He pressed the jar into my hands. "We came to give, not take."

"No big sacrifice on my part. In fact, come to think of it, I'd be glad to make a donation."

"I won't tell you what Harold would say, but let me see if I can explain it. You see, it's a Jesus thing. He sent us out like he sent the first disciples out, and He gave us some very strict marching orders. To take no money with us or pack any extra clothes, not even food. We accept what people give us - not rich people but poor people. It's them we go to. They are the ones to whom we tell the story. We eat what they eat and live where they live. If we travel from town to town we stay in their homes and baptize or marry, bury them or just tell them the truth. We accept what they give us and that is our wages. Our reward however, comes when we see the light that appears sometimes in their eyes."

"Very spiritual," I said. "Churches I've been to the pastors are usually a little more well fed, and they play golf twice a week with the big givers."

"Don't condemn them," Harold said from behind me. "We need the established church too. The problem is that unless you are poor you can't really accept poverty. It isn't part of your life. You need to live it day to day in order to love the poor. You need the frustration, and the faith to overcome it. We don't envy the golfers." He appeared slightly more subdued after the baptism.

"I see," I said, but I wasn't sure I did. "Time for me to get going. It was quite an experience to meet you."

Albert escorted me through the hallway to the outer door. Harold took my hand with both of his and said, "I wish you all the best and hope you can someday think kindly of us. We don't want anything. Really."

"Yes," I muttered. "Of course."

Albert laid a hand on my shoulder and said, "God bless you."

I went quickly out the door into the blazing sunshine. I heard the latch click behind.

When I approached my car there was a beggar, attracted to cars as they are, waiting to tell me: *I washed your windshield, guarded your car.* The hand comes out. This beggar was the usual street deviant, an ugly, ragged fellow, barefoot and filthy, flashing the cunning, submissive smile common to beggars. That alone infuriated me, and begging itself has always seemed to me a kind of sanctimonious entitlement. It must take faith, at least. I turned the lock.

"Por favor," the beggar said. "No one has come near this little truck."

I opened the door and got in. It was stifling and I rolled the window down.

"One peso," he said.

It was a firm practice I'd held for many years - don't encourage them. There were plenty of jobs. It was a growing economy. I started the engine.

"Maybe you have change in your pocket?"

"What's that you're holding in your hand?" I asked him.

"A thing," he said. "A thing to clean your windows."

"It's filthy."

He looked down at the rag, fingered it with his dirty hands and said nothing.

"Do you like peanut butter?" I asked suddenly.

"Peanut butter?" he repeated. "What is that?"

"A kind of food," I said, and handed him the jar. "Here. Enjoy yourself."

I glanced in the mirror as I pulled away and he was still standing there examining it, bewildered by this new misfortune.

Wet Passage

A blue morning and *Molly B*, a blue and white boat, made her turn below the headland. Not new or fiberglass, a wooden boat painted time and again to salvage her shrinking boards. There was rust on the screw heads and she made smoke as the young captain piloted her toward the dark blue water and deep trench for the deep dive.

It was a small crew that morning, only the two of them, the young captain and his divemaster. The captain was Australian and the divemaster from Kent in England and they worked well together but became adversaries in the bars after three or four beers. Most mornings they were hungover and quiet. Both held the tourists aboard in contempt, and told stories in the bars about them. In these stories the women were all sluts, the men insolent and gutless. The tourists came mostly from the American Northeast, Midwest and from Canada. Their white skin, flaming pink after two days, marked them as rubes and they were pitiful characters in the stories told in the bars.

The group that morning was private. All from a single dive shop in Minnesota. The shop's owner and instructor was Carl Boe and he was middle-aged and serious. The young captain and the divemaster were warned about him by their employers. Told to be polite and not to argue. Mr. Boe was thought to be humorless and demanding, but he paid cash.

Carl Boe hated the deep dive. The other dives were predictable, though he never relaxed on them. His divers - he thought of them as his - were often so entranced by the color, warmth, activity of the shallower reefs, they soon shot up all their film or sucked their tanks dry and it was over. Carl counted them again and again and relaxed only when he'd sent the last one to the surface. Afterward, left alone underwater, it was all he could do not to fall asleep on the warm sand.

There was a light chop to the water that morning too, and several of the lake divers feared heavy seas. Carl didn't smile at such foolishness because he'd heard it so often, and anyway he thought his divers were rubes too. But he liked some of them because he'd trained them and seen the sacrifices they made to learn. He knew most of them were there just once. They'd tell about it back home, show pictures at work, and next year go elk hunting or parachuting. A few others entered the water and were bewitched by this rambling, wet place that seemed to them wide and intimate at the same time. They found something relevant here, and he guessed they'd be about as successful as he'd been at finding out what it was. That did make Carl Boe smile, but it didn't show on his lips.

Because Carl didn't like the deep dive, he was fastidious in preparation for it. Fussy it seemed to the crew, but they made every attempt to soothe him. He'd gone over it with them before leaving the dock. He would go over it again now just before they arrived on the dive site.

"Only two of these people have been deep before," Carl Boe said softly, leaning on the captain's chair so his lips came close to the man's ear. "I'm not taking any chances. I want two stop bars. One at ten, one at twenty. Four tanks, two on each bar. Make sure there are regulators on them all. Had that happen once in Cozumel. Some idiot put the tanks over but forgot the regulators. Did he think a panicked diver was going to somehow take his own regulator off and attach it to another tank? Was he supposed to hold his breath all this time or what?"

The young Captain nodded, forcing his face to remain blank. "Don't worry," he said, keeping his gaze ahead through the windscreen. "This isn't Mexico. It's not our first deep dive either."

"So you'll have two bars and four tanks?"

"Yes."

"I'm easy to please, but I like to bring them down and bring them back up again. I don't want to leave anybody there."

"Hasn't happened yet."

"Always a first time."

It was good he'd been warned, the Captain thought. The man was an old lady.

Carl Boe wasn't fooled by the Captain's blank expression, nor encouraged by it. He was consistent in his dealings with them. Cared little for their opinions. When he returned next year, these boys would be gone to Hawaii or Truk or Cancun. He'd been straight with them - we all go down, we all come up. Every precaution is taken. If not, he fired them. He'd done it before. He thought by now he might even have a reputation. This was another thing that made him smile.

The deep dive was "around the corner" as they said here. Around the end of the island where the charts show the fathom lines squeezing together and the shoreline within eyesight of the deep trench. The trench itself fell away underwater as a sheer cliff from sixty-five feet to 1,875 fathoms - just over two miles. No one went to those depths of course, but the exhilaration of flying off the ledge, over the abyss and down into it 120 feet, was as close to space walking as possible on the planet. The highlight of the trip. For Carl it was a nightmare. The potential for disaster exploded exponentially in deep water.

Even so, he was no fool, and saved the deep dive for the end.
A climax to the week. A thrill to promote repeat business. The
other ocean dives that had preceded the deep dive prepared the
Midwesterners enough to prevent mishaps. So he hoped, since it
worked before.

The English divemaster - chubby, playful, handsome - would
give the dive briefing after the boat was secured to a mooring float
permanently anchored at the sixty-five foot site. The divemaster,
who'd made this trip hundreds of times, would lead them to the
edge of the abyss. Carl would bring up the rear. That way the divers
would be sandwiched between them as they swam out into the deep.

This was not overcautious. Deep, clear water is deceptive because
high underwater visibility makes *far* seem *close*. Divers can easily
turn a safe 120-foot dive into a deadly 160-foot dive where nitrogen
levels in their blood creates narcosis - rapture of the deep. They
become euphoric, unpredictable and reckless.

Carl was especially worried about Lester Hubres, a stubborn
seventy-three-year-old fixated on his body, his health. Lester
ate a special diet, packaged in leaky plastic containers, and in
exhibitionistic fashion, exercised throughout the day. On the flight
down from Minnesota, he'd changed clothes in his seat, pointing
out his flat, naked stomach to the nearby passengers. He talked
constantly about his physical accomplishments, which were
impressive, and often surpassed the physical accomplishments of
his children. His wife had died, because she didn't take care of
herself Lester said, and that left Lester with a taste for younger
women. His gnarly, arthritic hands found their way into places they
didn't belong and Carl was too often put in a position of having to
speak with Lester, who seldom contained himself in a dive boat
atmosphere of bosoms and bikinis.

Soon then, they'd endure the divemaster briefing, an opportunity
for wit, sarcasm, and rote warnings. The piña colada rules. Pay the

divemaster one piña colada for simple mistakes, two piña coladas
for serious mistakes, ten piña coladas for drowning. It never varied
day after day, year on end, and Carl Boe was sick to death of it.
Once when he was a little tight, he happened upon a divemaster in a
bar and told him he'd like to buy him a piña colada, then shove it up
his ass. Or maybe he'd dreamt it. He didn't get that drunk very often
because it made him forget and forgetting was always worse than
remembering.

The piña colada briefings were giggle makers and from them Carl
predicted which of his female divers would be sluts-of-the-week in
the bar stories. Divemaster conquests were bragged of openly. So
he fidgeted through the long briefings and the immature attempts
the divemasters made to impress their future lovers. He'd taken to
giving his divers private warnings so they knew exactly what he
expected of them. He couldn't police their morals, keeping them
alive was hard enough.

Lester was his main concern and he spoke to him before the
briefing started.

"Lester." He sat down next to the old man. "Deep dives at your
age aren't recommended. Sit this one out and help the Captain
handle the stop bars and safety tanks, okay?"

"I paid like everybody else," Lester scowled.

"I know, but nitrogen does some strange things to bodies as they
age. Why risk it?"

"I'm in better shape than you are, if you don't mind my saying
so." Lester had an infuriating pout. "Don't see that little beer belly
on me. I don't let alcohol pass my lips. I drink fresh fruit and
vegetables from a blender. Never sucked one puff of a cigarette."

"You're in great shape but this isn't about that. It's about nitrogen
and the way it's absorbed and released by your body."

"I'm no different from you."

"Yes, you are." Carl knew his voice was taking an edge and
did his best to sound reasonable. Not to lecture. "I hope I'm in as

good a shape as you when I'm your age, but I'll still be your age. Understand? For some reason nitrogen reacts more unpredictably in older tissue."

"Why?" Lester was fighting his familiar enemy, age. "Just tell me that."

"I don't know. Nobody knows. All we know, is it's not worth the risk."

"It's my damn risk! You can't stop me."

Carl could stop him if he wanted to, he thought. Yes, he could turn the boat around at any time, take them all back to shore and tell them to kiss off. He wouldn't do that, no matter how unreasonable they became or difficult to handle or how risky their behavior. Besides being his divers they were his customers. They had that power over him. A power he gave them for money.

"Okay," Carl gave in. "You're buddy will be Steve. Stick close to him."

"What's wrong with Sara Meyer?"

"Nothing. She's diving with her boyfriend."

Lester pouted. "She'd be better off with me."

"Just stick close to Steve and watch your air consumption." Carl stood to go. "Air disappears fast at that depth."

Lester ignored him. He was angry about Sara, who he'd been flirting with most of the week. Sara thought it was cute but her boyfriend was an insecure roofer in a muscle shirt.

Carl was thirsty. The crew had a dirty plastic cooler strapped to a stanchion opposite the helm. There were paper cups in a plastic bag. Usually there was lemonade in the cooler but today they'd filled it with lukewarm water. Carl drank it to get the taste out of his mouth and the salt from his lips.

"Share?"

"Hi," he said to Anita Knapp, and reached for a clean cup.

"I'll use yours," she said, slipping it from his hand. "Fill it?"

She held the cup. He pushed the button. "I'm even more thirsty after the dive," she said.

"Me too."

She drank it off and crumpled the paper in her fist. "Want me to dive with Lester?"

"Steve's got him."

Anita wore black one-piece swim suits and never tanned. Her rich creamy skin was complimented by a smooth voice. "I don't mind."

"Let Steve do it."

"I was watching you," she said. "You were trying not to look mad."

Carl grinned. "Did I succeed?"

She shook her head. "No one else noticed."

"Lester did."

"Lester's all about Lester."

"So why would you baby-sit him then?"

"I'm a woman." She smiled. "I can keep him in line."

Carl had known Anita almost six years, since her divorce. She'd been married to a controlling man who kept her at home. Free, she'd done the first outrageous thing she could imagine, taken scuba lessons. He knew she had very little money and all year saved for this one trip. She was a paralegal somewhere, he recalled.

Several times Carl planned to ask her out. He admired her plainness, the small compact figure, but the disruption it might bring in his life frightened him. He wasn't surprised that she volunteered to help with Lester. It hadn't surprised him last year when she leaned against him and placed an arm so naturally around his waist and ran her fingers lightly along his side, and tucked them under his swimsuit waistband at the hip. Her fingers motionless and still, the way the sea is still, before losing itself to wildness. "You didn't come here to baby-sit," he managed.

"I don't mind. It's only one dive."

"Forget it." He glanced over her shoulder. "Almost there. I'm done working after today. You can buy me a beer at Etlee's tonight so I can smoke cigars and watch the sunset."

"No one goes to Etlee's."

"Yes, I know." He inhaled the greasy smell of her sunblock and bent down to kiss her nose. About time, he thought.

"Okay," she said. "Just me and you."

Carl didn't offer the short-handed crew any help mooring to the float. He snapped his BC to a fresh tank and walked along the lines of divers doing the same, offering words of advice or encouragement. The old decking blistered underfoot and the sun stood alone, blazing in a pale blue sky. He noticed Lester had washed and dried his new equipment the night before and placed it back into his dive bag so he could pull out each item in the order in which it was assembled. He'd refused to buy from Carl. Your prices are a rip-off, he'd told him. Carl recognized the discount brands. At least it was new, he thought.

After the decompression stop bars and safety tanks were lowered, Carl daydreamed through the briefing. The young Englishman had nine piña colada rules.

They hit the water around ten. The Englishman alone, ahead, then the rest two by two behind. Carl dropped in last, exhaling hard to sink beneath the surface and get them in sight. He did a count and watched as they teamed up and floated to the sixty-five foot reef from where they'd begin to go deep. It didn't seem the kind of day where things go wrong, not that that mattered, but you got a feeling about it sometimes, little things misfiring to warn you. The water was clear and the deep blue of the trench benign with color and the promise of life.

This was a place frequented by seven or eight hundred pound eagle rays. The giant creatures swim like motorized bats, gliding along the abyss at whatever depth they choose, sunlight reflecting from the spotted white of their broad backs. A shocking sight for the lake divers. A thing to talk about for years. Carl hoped they'd see the rays but oftentimes the divers simply missed them. They were too busy looking around to focus. He was no longer surprised when he reached the surface and asked, *Did you see the shark?* and met a circle of blank faces. *Was there a shark?*

There were no rays that day. Carl focused with his eyes and his intellect and prayed that today again they would all go down and all come back. He believed less in this as time passed. He was a logical man. One day his luck would run out and he'd lose somebody. He knew that would be the end for him.

At the bottom there was little time to waste. The divemaster brought his index fingers parallel and together, the buddy-up signal. He wanted them close. Carl hovered above, counting.

The divemaster swam backwards into the abyss, pedaling his fins and beckoning the divers with both arms. When they cleared the ledge and hung above the depths, he turned along the wall and lead them gently down into the deep blue that finished as black. Carl followed, calculating the distance between himself and Lester Hubres. Lester's arrogant recklessness was dangerous, but now he swam lazily alongside his buddy Steve. Lester pushed his fins back and forth rather than up and down. Poor fining forced him to work harder to keep up. He'd suck down his air and be sent to the surface all the sooner, and that pleased Carl.

Everything was in its place as he gazed down along the wall of the abyss and the hard and soft corals that clothed it. At one hundred feet he could easily see another hundred below. The wall went on and on into the blackness where no light has shown since the flash of creation, but here there was light and warmth and some color not yet faded to grays and blues. Grape-colored vase sponges grew in clusters of twos. Pale yellow fire coral and a pink anemone at the base of a long tube sponge surrounded by black coral whips swaying in the currents. Among these a squirrelfish darted. A small school of porkfish stood out from the corals.

At one hundred and twenty feet they leveled off. They'd remain at this depth only five minutes before beginning a gradual climb back to sixty-five. From there, ascend directly to the twenty and ten foot stop bars. Carl Boe demanded five minutes at twenty feet and ten minutes at ten feet. Outgassing the nitrogen took time and manifested differently in different tissue. They would decompress though they wouldn't exceed their no-decompression limits, because Carl was a cautious man. A prudent man. It gave him confidence. A cautious man isn't often wrong, even about deep water. He had instincts about it that couldn't be taught except over time. These instincts worked inside his head and allowed him to dive to the brink and swim back just in time, to turn from certain death to the warm light above. He didn't think of himself as a man who took risks though he understood the atrocity of failure, the unfathomable price of carelessness.

To his left and below, a wedge of eagle rays appeared and swam along the wall. Four together and two stragglers. They were coming up from behind, far enough out to maintain maneuvering room but close enough to spot a nice snack of shellfish. Carl fumbled for his knife so he could knock his tank with the handle and attract the diver's attention. He paused in the water to accomplish this and then swam on, moving slightly outside the group to help herd them closer to the wall if necessary.

A few divers heard Carl's tapping and turned to see him point out the rays. Most seemed oblivious and swam on. One of the more experienced swung his camera and its flash lit them for a second, then he turned again to swim on.

Carl had gone past the place where he was thrilled by rays. Not by whales or sharks or large eels. He marveled at them, admired their dominance as they passed, but he had become as much a part of the sea as they, and was comfortable with that. He took a lobster when he felt like it, shot a grouper when he was hungry for grouper. It was the last place on earth after all that a man could be what he was made to be, and even that was fast becoming a rare thing. People would soon be worshiping sharks as they did their puppies.

He counted the divers again. Counting wasn't easy because they moved and seldom stayed two by two.

He was one short.

He counted again.

He was one short again.

A missing diver is usually at the surface. Carl craned his neck. He saw no one. He counted again and searched below, left and right. He'd taken his eyes off them to view the rays and handle the knife. Moments. The only place he hadn't looked now was behind him. It seemed impossible and he shivered with dread.

Carl spun in the water. At first there was nothing and then he saw fins no more than five or six feet above his head. Someone was dangling there. A woman. The one Lester had been pestering. Sara. Eyes wide, she pointed at the disappearing rays. They had excited her and she'd somehow managed to swim around behind him. Carl's heartbeat slowed again and he signaled for her to rejoin her boyfriend. It was easy to forget how careless they were, how oblivious to the trench above which they hung like ripe mangos in the wind.

Carl counted again when she'd rejoined the group. Again he was one diver short. He thought he might be going crazy until he saw Steve pointing down along the wall where Lester Hubres was descending feet first into the gloom.

It was a conscious decision. Later, some said he'd followed his instinct. Not true. Carl Boe decided without emotion or fear or even excitement. He pulled the fin of the diver nearest him and pointed to the divemaster, giving the man a thumbs up to return them to the surface. Then he swam down along the wall to bring Lester back.

He approached Lester as one overtaking a moving vehicle - not suddenly, but gaining steadily. His senses were heightened and his mind calculated the risk factors of time and depth even while the more practical concerns dominated his conscious thoughts. He had to stop Lester's descent immediately and bring him back slowly regardless of what he knew would be a critical shortage of air.

He noticed how Lester held his finger firmly on the button that deflated his buoyancy compensator. Lester had extended his left arm overhead to vent air from his BC hose. Air that kept him from free falling into the abyss now escaped to the surface. As he fell, water pressure created a negative buoyancy that was all but impossible to overcome even by a combination of strong swimming and inflation of the BC with tank air. At some point the physics assumed the certainty of death. From that critical depth there was no return.

Carl listed the tasks ahead. Remove Lester's grip on the deflator. Inflate Lester's BC and his own. Swim hard and encourage Lester to do the same.

He had no time to glance at his depth gauge but he guessed their depth at around one-seventy or one-eighty, and that was close. At 297, the oxygen level in compressed air becomes toxic and both of them would be poisoned by their own breathing air. Shortly after that, they would die, extreme negative buoyancy carrying them into the greater depths. They would remain there, preserved by the cold, for years or until something ate them.

He closed the distance then and wasted precious seconds signaling to Lester, who was in a narcosis stupor - eyes vacant, mouth slack around his regulator mouthpiece, fingers frozen in his last conscious act of deflating his BC to descend.

Carl gripped Lester by the shoulder harness, pulled him close and inflated his own BC to slow their descent.

At first this seemed to fail, but then slowly they began to decelerate. If he pried Lester's fingers loose from the deflator they had a chance. Maybe he could even swim them up by himself. They would gain buoyancy as they ascended and air expanded in the BCs.

He snatched the deflator and pulled at it to release Lester's grip. Lester held on. He hooked his left arm around Lester's left arm and sought leverage to twist it away. Somehow Lester held on. The old man's arm was strong. He pried at the fingers and they were like the roots of an old tree. He let go with his left arm and punched Lester in the stomach.

Punches are slow and clumsy underwater and Lester took no notice.

Their descent was accelerating again.

Carl reached for his knife. He used the tip and tried to pry Lester's index finger from the deflator button. If he moved it, he could hit the power inflator and that would be enough. He didn't want to cut Lester.

The old man was conscious at some level. Carl pried with the knife. Lester strengthened his grip.

How far had they fallen? Another forty, fifty feet? It seemed darker. Carl was fighting laughter and realized he'd been talking to the finger. Nitrogen levels in his blood were making him silly, slowing his reaction time, fogging his mind.

"Finger, finger. Dirty finger. Finger, finger. Bony finger." There was a tune too, and he wanted to rhyme something with finger. What rhymed with finger? Binger? Dinger? Linger? That was the word. Linger.

Carl carried an expensive, stainless steel knife and kept it sharp. He'd cut the finger off and put it in his BC pocket. Lester could have it back later.

Lester's finger didn't have a great deal of flesh on it and the blade went through easily, hanging up on the bone. Carl turned the knife and used the serrated edge. It cut bone as quickly as rope. It seemed to Carl that this was an amusing circumstance, possessing a knife almost tailor-made to do fingers. He wondered how many fingers he might someday be forced to cut off. Hundreds maybe. A thousand. He was laughing again.

The finger didn't come off neatly and he thought that Lester was watching him, though that didn't seem likely since the old man hadn't made a sound or even struggled. He just held on to the deflator, which in the end helped Carl with his sawing.

There was blood in the water now. It was green from lack of oxygen and thick, almost rubbery. Maybe they'd escape this and then sharks would eat them. Carl laughed in a deep and choking way.

With the finger gone, Carl closed the deflator valve and pressed the power inflator. The sound of air hissing from Lester's tank seemed loud at first and then grew soft until it faded to a whisper. Carl laughed again and picked up Lester's pressure gauge. The needle had pegged at zero. Lester was out of air. The irony was too much for Carl and he shook with laughter.

He should swim. Why not? He'd make it if he ditched Lester. He'd been in tighter spots than this.

In the Red Sea.

He nearly drowned in the Red Sea. Down to the sea in camels. He saw divers, legions of them, galloping across the sand dunes on camels, tanks on their backs, turbans round their heads, masks keeping the sand from their eyes, snorkels flapping. Galloping down to the Red Sea. He saw the sand fly from the hooves of the knock-kneed beasts.

They were deep now. The color along the wall gone to gray. It was quiet and he felt how separate they were from everything. Somewhere they'd crossed a threshold into another place which he didn't think had a passage back to the light from where they'd come. He didn't care much about that because the new place was made of a soft dark flannel, wrapping him close.

He did swim though. The muscles in his legs seemed thinned to flat bands by the water pressure, yet he felt strong and joined to this new place. He stared at the wall. He was moving down not up.

Lester was dead and they were very deep.

He was breathing okay but it made lots of noise. The bubbles ran past his cheeks and danced away toward a surface that no longer related to them. Maybe he should leave Lester there and swim back. It was Lester, after all, who carried him deeper. When ships sank he wondered if the people floating to the bottom of the sea felt as he felt, or did they just inhale water and die. If they died like that, then he might be one of the only people in all of human history to sink this far and be aware of his surroundings. An awareness that wasn't particularly insightful, he thought.

Lester didn't look very dead, as freshly drowned people have a talent for. His eyes had closed but his jaw hadn't gone slack nor had he loosened his four-finger grip on the inflator. What happened to the finger, Carl wondered? He wouldn't have thrown it away. Absently, he patted his BC pockets. There. In the left one. He thought then about putting it in Lester's pocket but that didn't seem necessary and he decided to keep it.

The idea of letting go of Lester came back again but they'd been together so long now that he didn't want to leave him there alone. He knew about Lester being dead but hadn't they shared their descent? Did he just throw Lester away now because he'd died?

They were falling and it no longer seemed like falling. More like riding in something smooth and safe. Something that took you so deep you didn't need to turn back. Carl was content. He hadn't left anybody behind or appeared on the surface without Lester, but obeyed the tenet of the sea and unspoken law of his profession. His mind cleared. A wise man said that death was dimming the lamp because dawn had come. Below he saw only darkness.

The nitrogeon rush came again. He relaxed into it, just he and Lester and Lester's finger, bridging the wet passage. Carl Boe smiled once more.